Cooking Wit

Food and Memories
From the Swarthmore College Class of '76

FALL 2021 REVISED EDITION

Cooking With Us: Food and Memories From the Swarthmore College Class of '76

ISBN 978-0-578-31645-1

Welcome!

It's odd to write an introduction to a "revised edition" so soon after we sent out the first edition (albeit in pdf form) to the class, but it seems appropriate nonetheless.

Looking back with a certain amount of nostalgia, the series of virtual events we held during the pandemic lockdown to celebrate our class reunion was a wonderful way of reconnecting with old friends, and staying in touch with a community that has thrived for nearly 50 years (we're counting back to freshman year). But we suspect that your lives, as ours, are adjusting to the new normality, at least in terms of being busier socially and getting out of our homes more. Last spring seems quite far away, yet it remains ever present in our hearts.

We intend this revised edition of the class cookbook to be a permanent souvenir of one of the strangest years of our lives. Many of us feel that, in the absence of other activities, our days were spent thinking about food, planning food, acquiring food, preparing food, consuming it, and then beginning all over again (and only half-jokingly so). Maybe that's a bit extreme, but if this cookbook serves both to memorialize the pandemic ridden years of our 45th reunion (2020-2021) and to showcase the togetherness of the Class of 1976 and our Swarthmore community, then it will do. And, as we found out, there is nothing better than sharing food to help bring us together!

In this second edition, we have added a few more stories and one or two recipes that had fallen through the cracks. We enlisted the help of a wonderful professional graphic artist – thank you Susan Spangler – to redesign the book and make it a little more usable. We hope you try some of the recipes out, and if not, we hope you display a copy of this book on coffee table (or in your library shelf behind your Zoom screen). Please think kindly and fondly of your classmates who have shared their stories and recipes with us, and those who have eaten them.

Stay well and well fed until our next gathering!

Bruce *Petrina*

Bruce Robertson & Petrina Dawson

Book Design: Susan Spangler, www.susanspangler.com

Contents

Pizza, Pasta & Dinner 46

Bread, Biscuits & Desserts 61

Drinks 74

What we *really* ate at Swarthmore

Sharples Memories

An English perspective, Ian Chitty

At Swarthmore it was always Steak night- Saturday as I recall, and Clam Chowder with real grit included for authenticity.

As I recall, the catering was provided by a company called Saga (disparaged by two guys I had as guests on WSRN FM whose names escape me) as "The Saga Food Colouring Company" (please note UK spelling). There was also always the issue of Union approved horrid tasting lettuce, if you remember.

The food for me at Swarthmore was great - coming from a British University where we were all on Government grants to attend- and where the Universities were seen as government institutions and where the meals seemed like an extension of school dinners- unless you wanted to be poisoned by a colleague cooking in the dorm kitchen, or resort to the Fish 'n Chip van that arrived around 10 PM in the Students Union car park.

The Wizard of OJ, Karl Weyrauch

I played multiple roles on the food service side of Sharples as a way to earn money for textbooks etc. I worked on the dishwashing line, the janitorial service and was even the Host of "Steak Night" special dinners on occasion, escorting students to their specially-decorated dining tables. On the morning breakfast shift for several semesters, I filled the role of "Beverage Attendant." This job entailed making sure the coffee and tea dispensers were operating to maximum capacity, the milk dispensers topped-up; and of course, that the orange juice machine was always freely flowing with re-constituted frozen orange juice concentrate.

I thought it would be fun to wake people up with a quirky quote as they filled their glasses with OJ and so I would look up suitable quotations from Bartlett's that referenced such aquatic verbs as "Flow", "Gush", "Stream", etc. I wrote the quotes on 3 by 5 cards and taped them to the OJ machine. I found a food service hat somewhere and on it I wrote my own job title, "The Wizard of OJ," substituting a "J" for "Juice" instead of the "Z" in "OZ" and wondering if any of the sleepy folks shambling into Sharples for breakfast would take note. I wore my hat and enjoyed the jaunty way it set off the rubber apron I had to wear to keep dry from the spills of all those beverages!

I am delighted that somehow that silliness connected with the universe, and that today you've given me the chance to recall those glory days. It was a sticky job, because the orange juice machine needed to be rinsed out with each refill, and after standing partially-full and partially empty for half a shift it would accumulate a film of orangey pulp that needed to be rinsed away before refilling. I am happy to report, too, that my experience in Sharples paid dividends when I participated on the Pomona College exchange semester because I was easily able to get a job in the food service there, as well as at a variety of restaurants and food service joints after that.

Random Food Memories, Niley Dorit

At least one of these might be true but if not, blame it on my senior moments! There was a guy in Wharton (Jim Govatos??) who used to make killer pizzas every weekend for no particular reason. And they were superb. He (or whoever made them) handed them out on my floor with no explanation. There were just "there" and we just "loved them."

Then there was Matt Reckerd (sp?) who I think was from hills of Kentucky and he brought back freshly hunted rabbits after returning from a holiday. He cooked them in a stew... Again, in Wharton. Never having tasted rabbit, I gave it a try. The rabbit was fine, but who knew buckshot might be lurking in the meal? . . . and it was. Oh my!

For some reason we had Cornish game hen in the refrigerator in Sharples. Someone "borrowed" them - lots of them - and brought them to Mary Lyon and we had a great feast at a huge table. Someone in ML knew how to prepare and present them like we were in a Michelin starred restaurant. Again, a college culinary highlight that I will never forget.

Last of all, Geoff Troy ('75) and I would go to the market and get great steaks. At night we would run like hell through the darkness, across the terribly dangerous railroad trestle, on the lookout for an oncoming train light! Safely across the ravine, we would find a spot in the woods, build a fire, BBQ the prime ribs, drink wine, and have our 2-hour woodsy sabbatical in the midst of our stressful academic reality. Then we would run back across the killer trestle in the dark of night, having cheated death and homework for yet another day, back to our dorms!

Catherine Lucas, The Palace Guard

Sharples – In & Out

Learning to Cook On Our Own

Oatmeal Pancakes from Lise Weisberger

Carol Swingle

My mother didn't really know how to cook. (Neither did her mother.) My mother fed her husband and seven children but I never saw her dice an onion, sauté vegetables, or make a sauce. We had hamburgers and hotdogs, plain Minute Rice, frozen vegetables that were boiled or steamed, fresh corn on the cob, pot roast, etc.

The most exotic she got was tuna casserole (made with Campbell's Cream of Celery Soup) and Chun King Chop Suey from a can with the little crunchies sprinkled on top.

So in college my friend Lise Weisberger taught me a little bit about cooking. The first time I lived on my own, in grad school right after graduation, I was a vegetarian and had a roommate who knew how to cook. So for three years I cooked nearly everything from scratch—spaghetti sauce, bean soups, yeast breads, etc. "Recipes for a Small Planet" and "The Tassajara Cookbook" were my staples. Then came marriage in 1980 to a carnivore from South Dakota whose mother was "Your Neighbor Lady," who had had a cooking show on the radio since 1940! (She went on to a 64-year career as a "radio homemaker.")

My husband had been cooking since he was 6 years old and loved to cook. Lise had given me some of her favorite recipes on index cards, and a little box to hold them, but gradually I did less and less until, within a few years, I did NO COOKING at all. As in:

- My children never saw me prepare anything more complicated than peanut butter and jelly.
- When I was home for several years, as my children did when they were young, the first thing I asked my husband when he got home around 6:30 PM was, "What's for dinner?"
- Making a pot of coffee is now "too much cooking."

My recipes in this book are dedicated to Lise, my husband Todd (who cooks delicious vegetarian food for me now), my dear late mother-in-law, Wynn Speece, "Your Neighbor Lady," and my late sister-in-law, Dorothy Shields:

- Garbanzo Stew from Todd Speece
- Doey's Apple Cake Pudding from Wynn Speece
- St. Louis Salad from Patti G.

Ingredients

- 1⅛ cups milk
- ½ cup whole wheat flour 1 cup rolled oats
- 1 Tbsp brown sugar
- 2 Tbsp oil
- 1 tsp baking powder 2 beaten eggs
- ¼ tsp salt

Directions

- Combine milk and oats and let stand at least 5 minutes.
- Add the oil and beaten eggs and mix well.
- Stir in the dry ingredients until just moistened.
- Makes 10-12 four-inch pancakes.

The recipe box from Lise with three of the 20+ handwritten recipes she included

Maddie Wessel's Popovers

Marty Spanninger

The Swarthmore significance of this recipe is that it was shared with me by Madelyn Wessel - my super-brilliant roommate who is also an amazing chef and host. It's an e-z popover recipe– and I make it whenever I want to impress an overnight guest – or be an impressive house guest. It is also my go-to house gift – a popover tin – with the recipe. As in most things – the right tool for the right job is a requirement! *

Ingredients

- 4 Eggs
- 1 cup milk
- 1 cup flour
- ½ tsp salt

Directions

- Spray Popover tin with "Pam" or other non-stick spray.
- Put a small piece of butter in each of the muffin or popover "cups" and heat in oven until the butter is melted/bubbling.
- Combine milk and flour and salt in blender Add Eggs one at a time.
- Quickly pour batter into preheated popover tin with melted butter and bake in 375F oven for about 35–40 minutes until they're puffed and brown.
- Don't open the oven door to sneak looks in oven!

*You can also bake in muffin tins.

Ingleneuk Tea House Butterscotch Biscuits (Sheila Connolly)

Liz Cosgriff

"An inglenook is a nook on either side of a large open fireplace—a cozy place to sit and keep warm. I am not responsible for the odd spelling in this recipe, because it originated at the Ingleneuk Tea House in Swarthmore, Pennsylvania, a treasured local establishment that the same family operated for over 80 years. Alas, it is no more: the restaurant, which had grown substantially since its founding, was destroyed by fire in 2000. The structure survived but was returned to its original purpose as a single-family home. I lived two blocks down the street from it, and enjoyed its food more than once, as did generations of Swarthmoreans (including James Michener, when he attended Swarthmore College).

"Meals at the Ingleneuk were served family style, and featured hearty comfort foods. Only a few of its recipes have survived, including one for creamed spinach, which for some reason I've never understood my daughter really liked. The other is this biscuit recipe. The dough is definitely biscuit-like, but it's nudged toward sticky-bun status by the rich filling. These are definitely best when served quickly, just out of the oven; diners at the restaurant used to fight for them when the servers brought out a new tray." —Sheila Connolly

Ingredients

- 2 cups flour
- 2 tsp baking powder
- ⅔ tsp salt
- ½ cup vegetable shortening
- ⅔ cup whole milk
- ¾ cup firmly packed brown sugar
- 6 Tbsp salted butter, melted

Directions

- Preheat the oven to 425F.
- With an electric mixer, beat flour, baking powder, salt and shortening at low speed until combined (about 2 minutes). Gradually beat in milk until dough is firm enough to roll.
- In another bowl, mix brown sugar with melted butter until sugar is moist, but not runny.
- On a floured surface, roll the dough into a rectangle 8 in. wide and 1/4 in thick (the thinner the dough, the more "spirals" you'll get). Spread the sugar mixture over the dough.
- Cut the dough in half lengthwise to form two 4 inch strips. Lightly roll up each half.
- Cut each roll into 1/2 in slices (you should get 4-5 from each piece) and place the slices in a well-greased 9x9 baking pan. (Note: you'll have to squish the slices in—it will look untidy.)
- Bake in a preheated oven until the top is lightly browned, about 20 min. Remove pan from oven. Let stand for 5 minutes, then turn over onto another greased pan or serving plate (or you can serve them directly from the pan—nobody wants to wait!). Eat while still warm.

Pizza Rustica from The Vegetarian Epicure

Tim Nuding

This recipe is for memories of vegetarian cooking at Idlewild Lane, Media, PA! It's also delicious!!

This was counter-culture, save the planet and diversity all before its time. Several Swarthmore students lived in a communal house at Idlewild Lane in Media, PA in the 1974-1977 period. The household had about 8-10 people, combining students and local residents.

There was a mother who was a teacher in an alternative Quaker school who had two teenage children, a brother (carpenter) and sister (teacher) and 4-6 Swarthmore students who at various times included me, Mark Taylor '75, Barb Sieck '75, Rex Brigham '75 and a few others whose details I can't remember. There was a high level of tolerance for diversity of all kinds with the basic understanding that everyone pitched in and helped with the communal activities.

Each adult took turns cooking one day a week. We bought food at a local alternative co-op in bulk. As 2-3 of the residents were vegetarian, we cooked vegetarian about 3-5 days a week. I made tofu from scratch using dried soybeans--save the planet! (Still a good idea...and I still love it, having grown up in Japan.) Pizza Rustica – a hearty 2-crust pie – was a favorite of everyone, vegetarians and non-vegetarians alike, thus the recipe which I have used repeatedly over the years.

Living off-campus was a good antidote to the "pressure-cooker" atmosphere of campus and only a short train ride away!

Ingredients

Crust:

- 2 cups flour
- ½ tsp sugar
- ½ tsp salt
- ¾ cup cold butter, cut into pieces
- A few drops of lemon juice
- 1 Tbsp ice water

Filling:

- 5 eggs
- 1 lb. Ricotta cheese
- 2 Tbsp chopped onion
- 1 cup grated Parmesan
- Chopped parsley
- 2 Tbsp salt & fresh-ground black pepper
- 2 Tbsp olive oil
- 10 oz. tomato purée
- 4 oz. tomato paste
- ¼ tsp dried marjoram
- ½ tsp dried oregano

- ½ cup sliced ripe olives
- ½ lb. thinly sliced Mozzarella cheese
- 1 very large green bell pepper

Directions

To Prepare the Crust:

- Mix flour, sugar & salt.
- Cut butter into flour until mixture resembles small crumbs.
- Sprinkle a few drops of lemon juice over mixture.
- Blend in ice water a little at a time until mixture forms a ball. Only use what is needed.
- Roll into 2 disks, wrap in plastic wrap, and chill for 30-45 minutes.
- Prepare a 10-inch pie plate.

To Prepare the Filling:

- Preheat the oven to 425°.
- Beat the eggs, and stir in the Ricotta cheese, onion, parsley, Parmesan cheese. Season liberally with salt & pepper and set aside.
- Heat the olive oil in a small saucepan. Crush the garlic cloves into it and add the herbs.
- When the garlic is clear and begins to turn gold, stir in the tomato purée, tomato paste, and olives, and, once again, season well with salt & pepper.
- Slice the Mozzarella thinly.
- Seed the green pepper and slice it into matchsticks.

To Assemble & Bake:

- Spread the first disk over the bottom of the pie plate.
- Spread half or a little more of the Ricotta mixture over the bottom crust, arrange half the Mozzarella slices over that, then cover with half the tomato sauce, and spread half the green peppers on top.
- Repeat all the layers, and cover with top crust. Pinch the edges securely together and flute.
- With a very sharp knife, make 3 long, parallel slashes through the top crust.
- Bake for about 35-45 minutes or until it is well-browned. Let stand for 1/2 hour before serving. Serves 6 to 8 generously.

Me with Mark Taylor and Barb Sieck (Taylor) in the double exposed background

Annie's Cheesecake

David Newman

The food that made me famous at Swarthmore was Annie's Cheesecake – and it was named after an Annie I knew long before I met my to-be-wife at Swarthmore.

I still almost have the recipe memorized though it has been more than a decade since I last made it. I had the mixer and the springform pan and could get all the ingredients in the Ville.

The other real food memory, other than served meal, was dorm-room Passover Seders.

Ingredients

Crust:

- 1 stick butter
- 1 inner package + 3 graham crackers
- Pinch cinnamon

Filling:

- 3-8 oz packages cream cheese
- ½ pt sour cream
- 1 cup sugar
- 4 eggs
- Juice ½ lemon
- 1 pint sour cream
- ¾ cup sugar
- 1 tsp vanilla

Directions

- Preheat oven to 350 F.
- Beat softened cream cheese until soft. Add ½ pint sour cream, 1 cup sugar, eggs, and lemon juice, in order, beating well after each. Beat to death!!
- While beating, make crust: Crumble graham crackers. Mix w/ butter and cinnamon and press into springform pan (bottom and sides).
- Pour filling into prepared springform pan with crust.
- Bake at 350F for 45 mins. Do not peek. Turn oven off and cool very slowly – at least 30 mins in oven (do not open oven door) and 30 mins out of oven.
- Mix remaining ingredients, pour on cake, and bake at 450°F for 7 minutes. Turn oven off and cool slowly and completely -- you can open oven door or even take out of the oven if the room is not too cold.
- Just before serving, add topping of your choice, if desired.

Mrs. Lemon's Tunnel of Fudge Cake

Kathy Leser

I don't know if you remember her or not, but Mrs. Lemon was the admin in the Career Planning and Placement office on the 1st floor of Parrish East. She was such a warm and caring person, and loved to bake. Her desserts and sweets were legendary.

Among students whom she knew well, she would offer to bake something for you for your birthday from her assortment of recipes. Far and away the most favorite requested by students was her tunnel of fudge cake. I do have that recipe, but it calls for a box of frosting mix which I believe is no longer available in grocery stores (it's been replaced by those cans of prepared frosting).

Steve Mattingly asked me if I had Mrs. Lemon's recipe for a cake that includes yoghurt, and I do have that one. I also have recipes for a pumpkin cake, an applesauce cake, and lemon bars. I would be happy to share any of these recipes.

Ingredients

- 1½ cups soft butter
- 6 eggs
- 1½ cups sugar
- 2 cups flour
- 1 package fudge frosting mix
- 2 cups chopped walnuts

Directions

- Preheat oven to 350F
- Cream butter and sugar
- Add eggs, one at a time
- Add flour, frosting mix and walnuts
- Pour into 10-inch tube pan

Revised Versions

I made this multiple times over the years, at least until the packaged frosting mix was no longer available. It has a really gooey center, very similar to the chocolate lava cakes that were popular a few years ago. Am thinking I will give the revised version a try. You can never have too many chocolate dessert recipes... :)

- Substitute Jiffy Chocolate Fudge Frosting Mix; check the temp and don't cook longer than 60 minutes.
- Let the cake cool in the pan for 2 hours, then remove and cool completely.
- Or try Pillsbury's fix: https://www.pillsbury.com/recipes/tunnel-of-fudge-cake/8d3b4927-2f71-41a3-9dab-7750f045f252

Mrs. Lemon's Tropical Cake

Kathy Leser

Ingredients

- 2¼ cups flour
- 2 cups sugar
- 3 large eggs
- ½ lb butter (softened)
- 1-8oz carton yogurt (pineapple-orange, orange, lemon, etc.)
- ½ tsp baking soda
- ½ tsp salt
- 1 tsp orange or lemon peel
- 1 tsp vanilla extract

Directions

- Put all ingredients in bowl and beat at medium speed for 1 minute and high speed for 3 minutes. Pour into 9" square pan, 2" deep, lined on bottom with parchment paper and greased.
- Bake at 350F for one hour.

Shirley's Famous Brownies

Rhonda Resnick Cohen

I grew up in Havertown, which is only about a 20 minute drive from the College. Although I loved the College from the minute I first visited the campus, I was worried that it was too close to home and that my parents would not be able to give me the space that I felt I needed. After much discussion, my parents and I agreed that they would act as though I were living 1000 miles from home. My mother was true to her word and wrote letters to me even though it was a local telephone call between Havertown and Swarthmore. When my mother decided that I might like a little taste of home, she baked a batch of her famous fudge brownies. She knew that she was not allowed to drive to Swarthmore to drop off the brownies. Instead, she went to her local post office (this was well before the advent of Federal Express). She felt that she needed to ship the package special delivery and special handling so that I would get it before the brownies spoiled. After calculating the postage for sending the package, the clerk at the post office said, "Lady, for this much postage you could take a taxi cab to Swarthmore and back." My mother replied, "I can't – my daughter is independent." Thus began the tradition of my mom sending me care packages of brownies every few weeks through the mail. My friends and I always enjoyed the brownies (and I still admire my mom for her restraint in keeping our bargain).

Ingredients

- 4 squares (4 oz.) unsweetened chocolate
- ¼ lb. butter
- 3 eggs
- 2 cups of sugar
- 1 cup of flour
- 1 tsp. vanilla

Directions

- Melt chocolate and butter in double boiler.
- Mix eggs, sugar, flour and vanilla. Add chocolate mixture.
- Bake in greased 8x8 pan at 350 degrees for 35-40 minutes (do not overbake!).
- Let cool. Cut into squares.

Family Food

Wacky Cake

Karl Weyrauch

I am forwarding this photo of a recipe for "Wacky Cake" that has been in my family ever since I was a baby. My mom would always make me a wacky cake as a birthday cake when I was growing up. This pictorial depiction hangs by our kitchen now. It was drawn by Kanako Watanabe, the daughter of my wife's Japanese pen pal who came to live with us for about a year and learn English.

She loved wacky cake so much that she turned the recipe into a work of art, that doubles as a functional reminder of the correct proportions to use whenever we want to whip up a batch for a special celebration.

Ingredients

- 1 cup sugar
- 1½ cups flour
- 4 cups cocoa
- ½ tsp salt
- 1 cup baking soda
- 1 Tbsp vinegar
- 1 cup cold water
- ⅓ cup oil

Directions

- Sift sugar, flour, cocoa, salt & baking soda and pour into ungreased baking pan.
- Mix in vinegar, cold water & oil. Stir until smooth.
- Bake at 350° for 30-35 minutes.

Grandma Mollie's Chopped Eggplant

Dave Scheiber

My Grandma Mollie was famous (in our family, at least) for her homemade blintzes, bagels, walnut cake, and a vast variety of other delicious dishes. But chopped eggplant, a recipe handed down from her family in Rumania, was her pride and joy. Mollie was ten when her family crossed the Atlantic Ocean to Ellis Island, and she worked hard to attain the American dream – excelling in school, contributing her factory wages to support her family starting at age 13, earning her high school diploma and Bachelors and Masters degrees after her children were in school.

Preparing chopped eggplant – patlagele vinete, or "purple tomato" – was one of the few ties she preserved to the hard life her family had endured in Bucharest. She whipped it up to serve with crinkle-cut carrots and radish roses when anyone looked like they might need a tasty treat to tide them over till dinner. She even made it to serve at Janie's and my wedding reception, when she was well into her 80s, frightening everyone when the smoke from the roasting eggplant set off the fire alarm. But once the smoke had cleared, she was back at the stove, determined as always to bestow her special dish – and her everlasting love – on us all.

Ingredients

- 1 good-size purple eggplant, no firmer than bread to the touch
- 1 green bell pepper
- ½ an onion
- Fresh dill to taste
- ½ cup of Mazola oil
- Garlic clove
- Salt to taste

Directions

- Place eggplant directly on the burner over medium flame. Turn with a fork until skin is entirely blackened.
- Test with knife for softness all the way through.
- Peel off burned skin with sharp knife under cold water tap until surface is entirely clean.
- Place cooked, cleaned eggplant in colander and press with a heavy weight to drain all the liquid from the eggplant, and then chop it.
- Roast the green pepper on the burner until it is fully blackened. Then flatten the pepper and scrape off all the burned skin, and chop it.
- Grate the onion, mince the garlic clove, and chop the dill.
- Combine all the ingredients in a mixing bowl and salt to taste.
- Cool and serve on rye or pumpernickel squares or crackers. Enjoy!

Danish Rye Bread (RugBrød)

Cynthia Rasmussen

I grew up spending every summer with my Danish grandparents, and in that household breads had some substance to them, dense enough to stand up to an open face sandwich, and rich with undernotes of rye and pumpernickel.

For nine generations, my people were tailors to the Danish king in Copenhagen. Unfortunately, so family legend has it, the King considered it such an honor to tailor for the royal house that he never paid his bills.

So sometime in the early years of the 20th century, my grandfather and his dad immigrated to America to make their fortunes. They opened a tailor shop in a little town in upstate New York, among a merry colony of Danish ex-pats. To this day, the sound of spoken Danish makes me wistful.

Ingredients

- 2 cups lukewarm water
- 2 tsp dry active yeast
- 2 Tbsp sugar
- 2½ cups dark rye flour
- ¾ cup all-purpose flour
- 1¾ cups cracked rye berries (very briefly pulse whole rye berries in a strong blender or food processor until they're broken up into coarse pieces OR smash them in a heavy-duty bag with a meat mallet or other heavy object – if you can't smash the rye berries soak them in water overnight and make sure you leave the bread soak for the full 48 hours)
- ½ cup whole rye berries
- 1¼ cups whole flax seeds (or in a pinch, more pumpkin, chopped almonds or sunflower seeds)
- 1⅓ cups sunflower seeds or combination of sunflower seeds, pumpkin seeds and/or chopped almonds
- 3 tsp salt
- 1 cup dark beer (or ¼ cup brewer's malt syrup or dark corn syrup or molasses and ¾ cup milk or water)
- 1 cup buttermilk or kefir (vegan: 1 cup almond milk mixed with 2 tablespoons cider vinegar) (or 1 cup milk with 2 tablespoons of vinegar)
- Traditional rolled oats for sprinkling (optional)

Directions

- Stir the yeast and sugar in the lukewarm water and let sit for 10 minutes until the yeast is frothy.
- Combine all the dry ingredients in the bowl of a stand mixer. Add the yeast mixture, beer and buttermilk. Stir to combine.

- Fit the stand mixer with a dough hook and knead on the bread setting ("2") for 10 minutes. The dough will be very sticky, loose and not remotely malleable (i.e., incapable of being shaped).

- Scoop the dough into a very large non-metallic bowl or plastic container with plenty of head space (the dough will bubble up). Cover loosely with plastic wrap and let it rest in a warm place (room temperature) for 24-48 hours, depending on how sour you want the bread to be (be sure to ferment it for at least 24 hours to ensure enough of the liquid is absorbed and 48 hours if you were not able to crack the rye sufficiently). If you're only letting it ferment for 24 hours, first soaking the whole rye berries overnight before using them (drain thoroughly).

- Line a 9x5x3 inch bread loaf pan with parchment paper and oil lightly. Preheat the oven to 350F.

- Scoop all of the dough into the lined bread pan, pressing down as needed. (It's a lot of dough but it will fit.) Brush the top with water and sprinkle over evenly with the rolled oats (optional).

- Bake on the middle rack until the center is done (about 120 minutes). For best and most accurate results use an instant read thermometer and aim for an internal temperature of about 205F degrees.

- Let the loaf cool for 5 minutes before removing it from the pan. Let the loaf cool completely before slicing. Keep stored in an airtight container, refrigerator or freezer if you know it will take you a while to go through it.

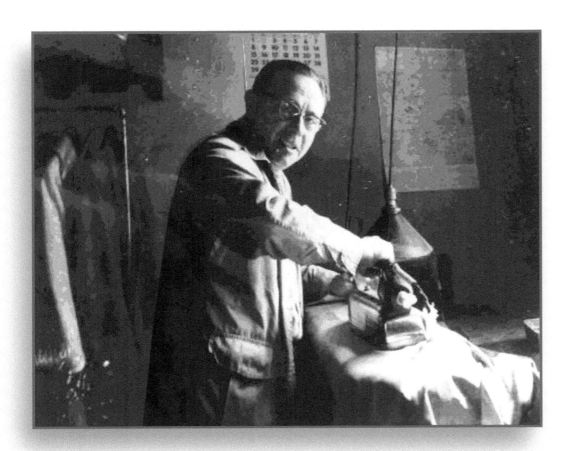

Niels Rasmussen

Gefilte Fish

Gilda Kramer

When I was young, my grandmother made fresh gefilte fish every week. My mother passed on to me my grandmother's recipe.

Every year we would host Passover for my family. Mom and Dad would come to visit days in advance, and we would cook all of the traditional family recipes, including Passover wine cake, turkey, brisket, tsimis, charoset, and of course gefilte fish.

Even though Mom and Dad are no longer with us, I have kept that tradition and each year I make gefilte fish from scratch and remember those special times with them

Ingredients

- 1 lb pike
- 2 lbs white fish
- 1 lb onion
- ½ lb carrots
- 2 eggs
- More onions and carrots
- Horseradish

Directions

- Use twice as much white fish as pike.
  I suggest 2 lbs white fish and 1 lb pike, boned, with skin, head, and bones packed separately for the fish stock.

- Scrape the extra fish from the bones and save it for the patties (a spoon works well, though Grandma used a knife). Make a stock using bones, skin, onions and carrots (slice carrots and onions). Use a lot of carrots and onions.

- For the fish, grind fish, onions and carrots in food processor. Use 1/3 as much onion as fish, and ½ as much carrots as onion. For four pounds of fish use 2 eggs plus salt and white pepper to taste. Chop eggs and seasoning into fish, and add a little water if too thick.

- I usually remove the onions and carrots from the stock, and save them to reuse use in a fish soup. Once the stock is made, slice more fresh onions and carrots and add the fish stock in a large pot.

- Bring stock to a boil. Form patties and cook in prepared pot with the carrots and onions and stock for about 2-1/2 hours after it starts to boil. After it starts to boil, lower flame, and cook on a low heat. Remove, place on a plate, and let cook.

- Keep the fish stock after the gefilte fish is done. It makes a really nice base for fish soup. You can add the onions and carrots from the first round, too.

- After I take them out with a slotted spoon, I place them on a large plate, and decorate them with a piece of carrot taken from the stock (carrots are sliced on a diagonal).

- Serve with horseradish.

My Mother's Southern Seafood Gumbo

Alan Symonette

People say, "It's so good, it'll make you want to slap your momma." It's that good, but you would not dare slap my mother.

This was a special recipe for my family and me. First of all, this is not from New Orleans. My mother would remind us that we are Miamian and as a result we make gumbo too. She did not admit that her original dish was influenced by my godmother Kate Johnson. She was from Lafayette, Louisiana. My mother modified it because she did not like whole crab claws in the dish. She did not like to reach her fingers in the dish to crack open the claws.

My version was further modified by my high school friend Cheryl Judice – Powell. Cheryl is New Orleans Creole, and her aunt Gladiola would have these huge parties at her house. She would give you a bowl and put a whole chicken breast or thigh in it and you had to find a seat somewhere in the living room. I used to fly from Philly just for that party. I did the party thing eventually but skipped the chicken for the same reason as above.

After I graduated from Swarthmore and law school, Debra (Pinder) Symonette '78 and I settled down. I started cooking this for us and a couple of friends. After we had our children and started organizing family celebrations, this became the dish served on New Years' Day in celebration of the final day of Kwanzaa. We would come together to eat and engage in Kwanzaa libations.

This party grew to include our friends, Debra's relatives, our kid's classmates, and other hangers on. Over time the Gumbo Party grew.

On New Year's Day we had a Kwanzaa open house with Gumbo, Black Eyed Peas, Collard Greens, Ham, Turkey, and various side dishes for 50+ people. Seriously, people made sure they were on the list. At one point we offered it for a fundraising auction – I would come to your home, cook, and serve it with salad and bread for a dinner party of ten people. At most it sold for $1,500. Eventually as the kids got older, we slowed it down even though we had relatives show up unannounced for a couple of years.

When Debra passed over, I stopped making it for a few years but my kids, a few relatives and Vanessa's family got into it. For my kids its again mandatory for the New Year. It is a taste of home. So, it is back on the menu. This New Year we made it and due to COVID I packaged it and delivered plates to my kids. Sorry for the long story but it is part of Symonette DNA.

Here it is:

Ingredients

- ½ cup vegetable oil
- ½ cup flour
- 2 medium onions chopped
- 4 stalks celery chopped
- 1 small green pepper
- 1 clove garlic minced
- 1 lb okra sliced (fresh is way better)
- 1 Tbsp vegetable oil
- 1 qt chicken broth

- 1 qt water (That's a lie. My mother added this to sabotage her recipe to the church ladies. Try seafood or vegetable broth with a half cup of cooking wine.)
- ¼ cup Worcester sauce
- 1 tsp Hot Sauce or Tabasco
- ¼ cup catsup
- 1 small tomato chopped or 1 can of diced tomatoes
- 1 tsp salt
- 1 ham slice, chopped or 1 lb. smoked sausage (andouille or kielbasa)
- 1 bay leaf
- ¼ tsp dried whole thyme
- ¼ tsp dried whole rosemary
- ¼ tsp red pepper flakes
- 2½ lbs unpeeled medium or large shrimp (I peel 'em)
- 2 cups cooked chicken – chopped
- 1 lb fresh crabmeat
- 1 lb sea scallops
- 1-12 oz container fresh oysters (optional)
- Hot cooked rice
- Gumbo file' powder (optional)

Directions

- Combine ½ cup oil and flour in a large pot. Cook over medium heat, stirring constantly until roux is caramel colored (20 to 25 minutes). Stir in celery, onion, green pepper, and garlic. Cook an additional 45 minutes stirring occasionally.
- In separate pan sauté okra in one tablespoon of hot oil until browned. Add to roux, garlic etc. mixture and stir well over low heat for a few minutes. At this stage mixture may be cooled packaged and frozen or refrigerated for later.
- Add broth and next 11 ingredients. Simmer 2 ½ hours; stir occasionally to make sure nothing burns on the bottom.
- Peel and devein shrimp. Add shrimp, chicken, crab meat, scallops, and oysters, if desired during the last 10 minutes of the simmering period. Do not overcook shrimp. Remove bay leaf.
- Serve over rice. Add Gumbo file' powder.

Venison Tomato Stew with Olives

Petrina (Albulescu) Dawson

This is my mother's adaptation of the classic Romanian recipe for Beef Tongue Tomato Stew with Olives to accommodate my dad's love of venison. In addition, because game meat was rare in Romania during the communist regime (after all, you could not trust the proletariat with shotguns, could you?), all of my parents' friends were very happy when this was served at the large get-togethers instead of the traditional dish.

The olive sauce is probably the Romanian translation of the French "chasseur" or hunter sauce with a Greek twist, so it pairs well with any kind of game. The trick is to pre-cook the meat you decide to use just short of done so it only needs 20-30 more minutes to be cooked in the sauce without falling apart.

While I do not have a photo of my mom's venison dish, it would look a lot like the photo of the beef tongue dish that I have included.

Ingredients

- 2 lbs venison
- 1 onion (cut up)
- 2 medium carrots (cut up)
- 2 stalks of celery (cut up)
- 1-2 garlic cloves (smashed)
- 1 Tbsp kosher salt,
- Thyme, pepper
- Red wine (or a ½ vinegar, ½ stock mixture)

Directions

- Marinate venison in the refrigerator for a minimum of 24 hours in a corning ware dish with a lid or in a large 2.5 gallon plastic bag placed in a bowl, rotating from time to time.

Marilena & Peter Albulescu at their combined 89th and 88th birthday party in June 2017 (birthdays are two days apart)

- Cook the Venison

- Cut the Venison to "petit fillet" sizes 1-1.5 inch thick and roughly 4 inches in diameter. Sear the venison in a cast iron skillet then place in a pot with the strained marinade liquid.

- Add:
  - 1 onion (cut up)
  - 2 medium carrots (cut up)
  - 2 stalks of celery (cut up)
  - 1-2 garlic cloves (smashed)
  - 1 bay leaf

- Add water or stock to cover the meat and cook on low heat till tender.

- You can do this a few days ahead of time and keep in the refrigerator or a few months and freeze and defrost the day before you are ready to make your dish.

Final Preparation -- Cooking the Venison in Sauce

- Cooked venison "filets"

- 4 tbs oil

- 1 large onion, chopped fine

- 3-4 tbs tomato paste

- 2½ cups chicken stock and ½ cup wine (or 3 cups stock)

- 3 garlic cloves, sliced thinly

- 2-3 bay leaves

- 2 tsp fresh thyme, to taste

- 1 cup pitted kalamata olives (but you could use green olives too)

- 1 tsp peppercorns, optional

- Optional thickener: 2-4 tbsp flour (or cornstarch or tapioca flour if you want a gluten free dish)

- In a large skillet, heat oil on medium heat. Add onion and lower heat a bit (medium/low). Cook onion until real soft, stirring every so often for about 15 minutes or so.... you can sprinkle a bit of salt in this step if you like.

- In a medium/large measuring cup, add tomato paste, and 1 cup stock... you can add the thyme. Stir to combine.

- Remove skillet from heat for a bit and add tomato paste mixture to the cooked onion. Stir to combine, then add the rest of the stock and wine (about 2 cups). You can use only stock if you don't want to use wine (and check for acidity at the end, you might need a little more lemon juice).

- Add sliced venison, olives, sliced garlic, and bay leaves.... add peppercorns(optional). Stir. Increase heat and bring sauce to a boil, cover and lower heat to a simmer.

- Simmer sauce for 25-30 minutes... check sauce every so often and stir, making sure nothing sticks on the bottom while it is cooking.

- Season sauce with salt and pepper as needed... and thicken sauce if you feel it is needed with a bit of flour and water mixture or corn starch /water slurry; or tapioca flour/water slurry. Make sure you cook for at least 5 minutes after you thicken the sauce.

- At the end, "freshen" up the dish with a squeeze of lemon juice and a bit of fresh parsley, or chives.

- Serve with: mashed potatoes, egg noodles, crusty bread, rice, couscous, quinoa, etc. If you want to make the traditional beef tongue recipe you can check it out here:

- http://homecookinginmontana.blogspot. com/2013/01/romanian-limba-cu-masline-or-beef. html

Barbara's Brisket

Dave Scheiber

My mom, Barbara Scheiber, who passed away in March 2021 at age 99, prepared brisket according to a recipe with family roots that dated back to the turn of the 20th Century in the Lower East Side of New York. Inside Abramson's Strictly Kosher Restaurant, located at 106 East Broadway, Sarah Abramson, my dad's grandmother, did the cooking while her husband, my great-grandfather Joseph, ran the register and greeted customers. According to Sarah and Joseph's wishes, all of their children left the Lower East Side after they'd finished school.

My grandmother Augusta, Sarah and Joseph's youngest daughter, became a concert pianist and, after marrying my grandfather, bought a brownstone in Greenwich Village, where they raised my dad and his sisters. After Joseph Abramson died and the restaurant closed, Sarah joined my dad's parents in their Greenwich Village home and gladly shared the recipe with the family's live-in housekeeper, Anna Simpson. Anna added touches learned from her rural southern upbringing with a bit of sugar and honey, giving the brisket a distinctive flavor. And my mom made a point to learn it, adding modifications of her own, including when to add bay leaves, carrots, when to baste, how low to keep the flame, and more.

The result is Barbara's Brisket, though she would have been the first to pass credit to those who came before her dating back to Abramson's on East Broadway. Beyond its history, this recipe tale has a genuine Swarthmore connection: My father, Walter Scheiber, was a member of Swarthmore College Class of '44, marrying Barbara (Vassar '42) in 1948 after serving in World War II as a turret-gunner on a B-24. And the recipe now lives on in new generations with so many family memories.

As you can see, my mom didn't go in for cookbook-style measurements. She measured by taste, touch, look and feel. She'd want you to feel just as free as she did to proportion the ingredients according to your own and your family's tastes, as well – and most of all, to enjoy!

Ingredients

- Brisket
- Onions
- Carrots
- Potatoes
- Bay Leaves
- Chicken Broth (about a quart for each brisket)
- Red wine (at least 1/3 bottle for each brisket. Cheap wine is fine to use).

- Non-MSG tenderizer
- Honey
- Ketchup (about 1/3 container for each brisket)
- Garlic powder
- Kosher salt and pepper

Directions

- Preheat over to 250F.
- Cut the fat with sharp knife from both sides of brisket Wipe meat off thoroughly, rubbing fairly hard.
- To tenderize, pound the meat with a mallet or rolling pin
- Stab the meat with a fork on both sides
- Sprinkle water on the meat and spread it over the surface
- Cover meat thoroughly with tenderizer; use the tines of a fork to scrape it lightly into the surface
- Let it stand 5-10 minutes
- Dice the onions; Peel carrots, cut in 2-3 inch pieces; Peel potatoes – if large, cut in halves.
- Sprinkle garlic & a little pepper on tenderized meat, and lightly scrape it in with tines of a fork. Sprinkle on a little kosher salt. Note: too much salt at this point interferes with the browning.
- Cover bottoms of pans with oil; heat.
- While oil is heating, spread honey over the top of the meat.
- Sear the meat over high heat. Add more honey (and more oil if needed) when you turn the meat over.
- Add onions to the pans. Stir to keep from burning. Turn the heat down when the meat is browned.
- Cover pans tightly with heavy foil, and put them into the oven or on stovetop over VERY LOW flame.
- Mix chicken broth, red wine & ketchup to create basting broth/gravy. Keep hot while brisket cooks; add to meat during cooking time.
- After an hour, add the carrots & potatoes.
- Baste meat every hour until meat is tender (takes at least 6 hours, maybe longer).
- When meat is tender, take it out of oven and place in container for refrigeration. Remove the carrots and potatoes, and put them into a separate container.
- Pour cooked gravy to cover meat and refrigerate meat and vegetables overnight. Refrigerate remaining gravy.
- Remove fat from gravy the next day. Heat gravy. Slice meat into paper-thin slices, and warm it in the gravy. Add salt if needed.
- Reheat the vegetables in gravy in separate pan

Family Apple Pie

Debbie Vernon DiMicco

I grew up with this recipe. I made it for hosts when I was spending my junior year in Grenoble and when chaperoning trips to Alsace, France with my students.

I usually roll out the pie dough on wax paper and flip it into the pie plate...no such thing when I was in France, so I used newspaper.

Got high praise from Mme. Silvy in Grenoble who said "La pâte est très fine" (never mind the dough looked a bit like silly putty with some ink transfer....) and when in Alsace, that the method of making the crust and the crumble (cutting in with knives) was very German, so in Alsace I was right at home.

Ingredients

Filling:

- 4-8 tart apples (depending on how full you want the pie plate)
- ½ cup sugar
- 1 tsp cinnamon
- ¾ cup flour
- ½ cup sugar
- ⅓ or ½ cup butter

Directions

Crust:

- Prepare a pie crust (⅓ cup crisco, 1 cup flour, some salt) cut crisco into the flour and salt, add 3 Tbsp cold water, mix together, roll out into pie plate)

Filling:

- Slice apples and place into pie shell. Mix ½ cup sugar and cinnamon together, sprinkle over the apples. Cut butter, flour and second ½ cup sugar together, sprinkle over the apples.
- Bake at 375F for 10 minutes, lower to 350F. Bake until apples are soft and juices run.

Nancy's Nana's North Carolina Pecan Pie

Nancy McGinnis Jirtle

Bonnie Martin Maness (1898-1989), my maternal grandmother, wrote out her pecan pie recipe for me to take to college. She visited the Swarthmore campus once and sat in on a history class lecture by Mr. Bannister. The twelfth (and last) child of a Civil War veteran, she shared her own love for history by repeating the family stories I hounded her to tell.

Nana's pecan pie works every time. The ingredients are stirred or mixed on medium speed, poured into an unbaked 9" or 10" pastry crust (purchased or made using her recipe), and baked at 325°F for 50 minutes. The corn syrup brand she used was Karo, and her vegetable shortening was Crisco. I add the 1 tsp of vanilla flavoring, as the recipe notes you may do.

You can bake it a day or so before you need it or the day you need it. Be forewarned, however; once it is cut, it will disappear! If you freeze it, allow it to return to room temperature before serving. Some people like it heated and served with vanilla ice cream. I prefer it the way Nana served it – at room temperature without further adornment, the flavors speak for themselves.

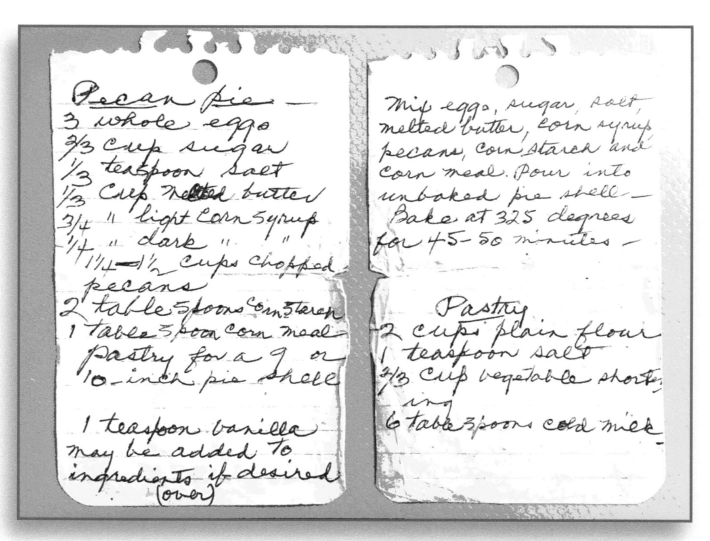

Bonnie M. Maness's handwritten recipe for her delicious pecan pie, 1972

Turta Dulce (Romanian Spice Cake) – Vegan

Petrina (Albulescu) Dawson

This cake is often translated as gingerbread, as it is ever so close! It is also very similar to the Moravian spice cookies recipes and many other "spice cakes." My grandmother used to make it often and it was one of my favorites sweet treats growing up. When I went back to Romania in 1992, I kept looking for it, but it never tasted quite the same as my grandmother's.

In January of this year, I started a quest to recreate the recipe: I had my trusted Romanian cookbook bible, Sanda Marin, with 4 recipes. I found another 4 or 5 on the Internet. My cousin's wife gave me two that my aunt used to make, and my friend from elementary school sent me one also. Some recipes had 5 eggs and honey, others had 2 eggs, milk, sugar and honey, some had chocolate, some had milk but no eggs, and some had butter. I made them all and only one tasted close my grandma's, even accounting for some faulty memory! It was the one with just oil and sugar: no eggs, no honey, no milk, no butter – the poor man's recipe.

Ana Radulescu at 88 in 1979

After my 5th attempt or so, my mom mentioned that my grandmother used to make Turta Dulce during the Great Depression and WWII, and she had a "war time recipe." It occurred to me that this recipe was likely the one she used during the communist era of shortages.

Ingredients

- 450 g all-purpose flour
- 250 g sugar (300 g if you like your cake sweet)
- 1½ cups water
- 2 Tbsp rum
- ¾ cup canola or vegetable oil
- 1 tsp baking soda
- 1 Tbsp cinnamon
- ½ Tbsp ground cloves
- 1 cup coarsely chopped walnuts
- ½ tsp ginger and ½ tsp nutmeg (optional and definitely not my grandmother's)
- 1 tsp orange zest or some candied orange peel (if you have it – grandma never did)

Directions

- In a small saucepan melt and burn to dark amber 150g of sugar and then pour the water over it to stop the burning. Take the saucepan off the stove, mix till all the burnt sugar is dissolved and then add the rest of the sugar and mix till dissolved.
- In a bowl, sift the flour, and add the sugar syrup slowly mixing well (you can do this by hand or in a mixer with a paddle). Add the rum, oil, baking powder, cinnamon, cloves and other spices if you decide to use them. Fold in the nuts and the orange zest or orange peel.

- Place in a well-oiled 9x13 pan (or a 1/2 sheet pan if you want thinner cake that you can cut into bar-like shapes) and bake at 350F till toothpick comes out clean (20-45 minutes depending on thickness).

- You can glaze with Royal Icing or use Butter Frosting, but we would just eat it the way it came out of the oven without any glazing ... barely letting it cool down!

- P.S. You can look up Turta Dulce on the Internet and find recipes for individual cookies or sheet cake with eggs and honey that are very rich and sumptuous. But they don't taste like 1968 communist summer!

Kentucky BlackBerry Jam Cake

Steve Mattingly

This was a Christmas tradition my mother got from her mother and I've continued with my family. The cake is best when it's well "aged" so I try to make it the Friday after Thanksgiving. I often continue to add bourbon while it is aging.

The black walnuts are an essential ingredient (order them on nuts.com). As a kid I remember gathering the nuts with their husk in and putting them in burlap sacks and have my father run over the bag several times to remove the husks. We then would dry the nuts and finally crack them open usually with a hammer. The nuts do not come out of the shell easily. It was a lot of work to get a cup of nut meats. If we got more as we usually did my mother sound add them to the Divinity candy, another holiday traditional item.

Enjoy!

Cake

Ingredients

- 1 cup butter
- 2 cups sugar
- 5 eggs
- ¼ tsp salt
- ½ tsp cinnamon
- 1¼ tsp ground cloves
- 1½ tsp ground allspice
- 3 cups regular flour
- 1 cup raisins or chopped dates (I prefer the dates)
- 1 cup black walnuts (check online to find them)
- 1 cup seedless blackberry jam
- 1 cup buttermilk
- 1 tsp baking soda
- 1 cup good Kentucky Bourbon

Directions

- Prepare 10 cup bundt pan spray with nonstick release
- Cream butter and sugar until light and fluffy, add eggs one at a time. Combine the flour salt and spices. Dissolve the soda in the buttermilk. Starting with the flour add alternately with the buttermilk.
- Quickly add the jam, nuts, and raisins or dates, Batter will be purple.
- Bake at 325F for 35-45 minutes, check frequently after 35 minutes and as soon as a cake tester comes out clean remove from oven. Cool in pan for 5 minutes, then turn out onto a cake plate. While cake is still warm slowly drizzle with ½ cup of the bourbon. Allow to cool completely and then drizzle the remaining ½ cup of the bourbon.

- Can be baked in three 8" cake pans, decrease baking time to 25-35 minutes, ice with a good buttercream or a caramel frosting.

Caramel Frosting

Ingredients

- ½ cup butter
- 1 cup brown sugar
- ½ tsp vanilla or bourbon
- ¼ tsp salt
- 2½ cups powdered sugar (approx.)
- ¼ cup milk or cream

Directions

- Melt the butter in a saucepan and brown sugar and salt. Cook over low heat stirring constantly for 2 minutes, add milk and continue stirring until mixture comes to a boil.
- Add sugar and beat till creamy, adding extra milk by drops until of spreading consistency. Quickly ice the cooled layers as this icing intentionally becomes hard.
- Only ice the middle and top of the cake as this icing is very sweet.

Golden Chocolate Cake

Debbie Vernon DiMicco

This is a bit of an undertaking, but delicious. It comes from my great grandmother Celia. My daughter, Gioia, insists that I make this cake for her birthday, and every year I complain that it takes all my pots and bowls to make. But I make it anyway.

It's two layers, with custard in the middle and a yummy frosting. It does get a bit leaky, I use the icing like mortar to plug the leaks.

But the goodness is in the eating, n'est-ce pas?

Cake

Ingredients

- 2 cups flour
- 2 tsp baking powder
- ¼ tsp baking soda
- 1¼ cups sugar
- 2 sq (oz) unsweetened chocolate melted
- ½ cup butter
- 2 eggs unbeaten
- 1 cup milk
- 1 tsp vanilla

Directions

- Sift dry ingredients, cream butter and sugar, add eggs and melted chocolate, add flour alternately with milk, add vanilla, bake in two pans at 350F approx 40 minutes

Custard Filling

Ingredients

- ½ cup sugar
- 1½ cup milk (heated in the microwave)
- 3 tbs flour
- 2 egg yolks
- ¼ tsp salt
- 1 tsp vanilla

Directions

- Put dry ingredients in top of a double boiler, add warm milk, cook over water stirring constantly, for 10 minutes (until good and thick).

- Pour small amount over 2 egg yolks, add to pot, cook another 2 minutes, add vanilla, cool.

Frosting

Ingredients

- 4 tbs butter
- ½ tsp vanilla
- ¾ cup + ¾ cup powdered sugar
- 2 sq (oz) chocolate
- 2 egg whites

Directions

- Cream butter, add ¾ cup powdered sugar and melted chocolate. Beat egg whites until stiff, add ¾ cup sifted powdered sugar, 2 tbs at a time. Add to chocolate mixture, fold gently until mixed.

- [Petrina suggests: Pipe a ring of frosting around the bottom layer of the cake to hold in the custard.]

- Put custard in the middle between the two layers of cake, then frost with the frosting.

Grama Vi's Dark Cut-Out Christmas (*or now, I say, whenever!*) Cookies

Julie Berger Hochstrasser

This recipe is from my mother's mother, my Grama Vi Trautmann. In the interest of historical accuracy, I have quoted the recipe below exactly as my mother gave it to me—in 1982, I see on the recipe card, when our first child was born and it was time to start making Christmas cookies with my own kids, as Mom always had with me.

But please do see also the footnotes with my own annotations. (N.B. No, you don't have to use LARD!)

And for further discussion of the connections with My Life After Swarthmore, see below that—hopefully with a plate of cookies to munch on!

Ingredients

- 1 cup lard (or other shortening — see note 1)

- 1 cup sugar

- 2 eggs

- ½ cup molasses

- 1 tsp [baking] soda [mixed] into

- 4 cups flour (about – see note 2)

- 1 tsp cinnamon

- ½ tsp cloves

- ½ tsp allspice (see note 3)

- Anise seed (ground) (to taste) or a few drops anise oil (Mom says 1 pkg.— you'll kind of have to play this by ear—try a tsp maybe. Oil or essence of anise is very strong—beware!) (see note 4)

Directions

- Mix, chill (see note 5)

- Roll out (thin as possible—tho' it makes a million! – see note 6)

- Bake. Frost. (see note 7)

- Enjoy!! Mom said dark was for animals, trees, people, toys, shapes. (see note 8)

- (The smell of these makes Christmas.) (see note 9)

Notes

1. I don't do lard — I just use straight butter. Mom's comment on the White Cut-out Christmas Cookies (see below) was "butter or oleo or half and half"— another blast from the past! Oleo???!

2. ...And THAT is the beauty (or the mild frustration) of ALL my Grama's recipes!! You simply add the right amount for the consistency of dough you know you need! Remember you'll add more

when you roll them out, and work it in as you do. I like to use at least some whole wheat flour (like up to half maybe even, especially if you have "white whole wheat"), along with unbleached white for the rest — because I like my cookies to be FOOD! — but be advised that they do turn out hearty that way. Grama wouldn't have done that—it's my Groovy Hippie Earth Mother Julie version.

3. Allspice is actually its own berry, but you can also replicate the flavor with equal parts cinnamon, cloves, and nutmeg. Funny that, while we did make gingerbread men with these, Grama's recipe doesn't include ginger!

4. I use the oil, and a few drops are plenty.

5. Again, like all her recipes—and, as I have since read, like all recipes back in the day when people actually knew how to cook, this leaves most of the details to your Old Wives' knowledge of how to make cookies: of course you know to cream the butter and sugar together, add the eggs and mix well, then the molasses; sift all the dry ingredients together and then mix gradually into the wet, mixing just until blended, since over-mixing wheat flour develops the gluten and makes the cookies tough. Right?! Back in the day, you just KNEW all that!

6. You'll find they do puff up quite a bit.

7. You really don't have to frost these—I think they're fine as is—but to decorate them, it's fun to make white icing and pipe it on so you can add things like red hots (for Rudolph noses, Christmas tree balls, gingerbread people's buttons, etc.), currants (for eyes), and so on, added while the frosting is still wet so they'll stick. Sky's the limit!

8. I also use her recipe for White Cut-Out Christmas Cookies, and as Mom reported: "White cookies for my mom were stars, stockings, wreaths, angels, bells." Happy to provide upon request. Their secret: wintergreen!!

9. Oh so true! But I consider this a very multi-purpose recipe: great for Valentine's Day, or Halloween (see photos), or if you just want molasses cookies, roll them into small balls, flatten with a glass dipped in granulated sugar, and they're good any old time! Molasses is a good source of iron, selenium, and copper, all of which make healthy bones! See what I mean? Cookies are food!

They started out as Christmas cookies, but they work for Halloween and for Valentines for kids and grandkids.

Reflections on Food, Scholarship and Life

Julie Berger Hochstrasser

Afew years after I graduated from Swarthmore, I was teaching art and music at a boarding school on a ranch in the Trinity Alps in northern California (and loving it! —but that's another story) when I saw a Time magazine cover about the "crisis in the liberal arts." However corny it sounds, I felt a calling. So precious to me was my experience at Swarthmore, I felt inspired to contribute to the perpetuation of the values and insights that liberal arts education could provide. Having majored in Art History at Swarthmore, I embarked upon an Art History PhD program at U.C. Berkeley.

Still torn between academia and studio arts, I initially thought my area might be Modern, but by my lights the most interesting thinker there at the time was Svetlana Alpers, so although I had already passed the language exams for German, French, and Italian, I thought, what's one more language? — and launched into 17th-century Dutch. A painter friend who was a prof at Santa Cruz called the Dutch Baroque still-life painters the heavyweight champions of the painting world, and little had been written on them at the time, so with my outside field as Anthropology, I wrote my (absurdly long) dissertation on Life and Still Life: A Cultural Inquiry into 17th-century Dutch Still-Life Painting.

When I landed a tenure track position at the University of Iowa in Early Modern Northern European Art, the book I wrote for tenure was one half of one of three sections of that dissertation: Still Life and Trade in the Dutch Golden Age (Yale University Press, 2007) explores the origins of various foodstuffs depicted in those sumptuous paintings, and (with true Swarthmore dedication to concerns of social justice) ultimately uncovers the appalling social costs of the luxuries depicted, in the exploitation perpetrated by the Dutch trading companies all across the globe. So for the ugly underbelly of the Dutch Golden Age, rife with stunning parallels to the present day in the way distant markets could enable consumers to remain oblivious to those true social costs, read the book, or I'll be glad to forward my cv with dozens more related articles and book chapters to keep you busy!

That work sparked The Dutch in the World, my subsequent project still ongoing today, which has taken me to key sites of early modern trade throughout Asia, Africa, and the Americas, investigating the artistic and cultural interactions that resulted from those early modern encounters. But for our present context, the more specific connection is the early modern trade in pepper and spices that drove the founding of the Dutch East India Company (Vereenigde Oostindische Compagnie or VOC), the world's first multinational corporation, and yielded wild profits that fueled the Dutch "Golden Age." Circuitous, yes, yet actually more substantial a connection than even I quite realized! Who would believe the drastic atrocities committed in the getting of pepper or salt, condiments that now sit out free of charge on restaurant tables throughout our country? Or likewise for the cinnamon and nutmeg that our local coffee roastery just leaves out for us in shakers on the counter?

Spiced cakes and cookies are still common fare in The Netherlands today, as my family discovered for ourselves during my Fulbright fellowship there, when my husband quit his job for the year to serve as Mister Mom while I did my dissertation research, and our three kids (then ages 4, 6, and 8) all went to Dutch school: yes we did indeed enjoy their (Dutch) spiced goodies. Ontbijtkoek or breakfast cake, with cloves, cinnamon, ginger, and nutmeg, is available in every grocery and convenience store, and we learned that the Dutch gave us not only Santa Claus (Sinter Klaas—though they put out their shoes on December 6 instead of stockings on the 24th), but also the very tradition of Christmas cookies, as Wikipedia attests: "The earliest examples of Christmas cookies in the United States were brought by the Dutch in the early 17th century."

Wikipedia's account further cites the role of Germany, which takes us right back to my Grama, who still spoke German with her parents, who had themselves come over from Bavaria. "Modern Christmas cookies can trace their history to recipes from Medieval Europe biscuits [sic], when many modern ingredients such as cinnamon, ginger, black pepper, almonds and dried fruit were introduced into the west. By the 16th century Christmas biscuits had become popular across Europe, with Lebkuchen being favored in Germany..." Gingerbread, in particular, "has existed in some form since sugars and spices were brought back to Europe, from soldiers in the Crusades. However, it was not until Queen Victoria and Prince Albert included it with a variety of other German Christmas traditions that the gingerbread cookies became primarily associated with Christmas."

And finally, bringing it right up to Grama's day, Wikipedia provided me with some fun-fact trivia regarding her recipes for "cut-out cookies," so thank you Bruce, for inspiring this little investigation: "Due to a wide range of cheap imported products from Germany between 1871 and 1906 following a change to importation laws, cookie cutters became available in American markets. These imported cookie cutters often depicted highly stylized images with subjects designed to hang on Christmas trees. Due to the availability of these utensils, recipes began to appear in cookbooks designed to use them. In the early 20th century, U.S. merchants were also importing decorated Lebkuchen cookies from Germany to be used as presents."

Grama Vi

Grama Vi was a wonder, and would have been the envy of any star chef today: as a younger woman she had taught all her eight younger siblings in the one-room schoolhouse in Forest Junction, Wisconsin, and sewed all their clothes.

Still when I knew her, which was into her eighties, she baked her own bread all year round, made her own jams and jellies, and for Christmas pulled out all the stops: besides the dark and light cut-out cookies, she made fudge (chocolate and divinity), "seafoam" (aka honeycomb), toffee (think modern-day Heath bars, only melt-in-your-mouth better!), hand-dipped chocolates (and

I have all those recipes too for anyone brave enough to try them!), and even (as my mother later wrote) while her own kids were young, also sewed a new dress for each of her three daughters for the holiday.

My mom is now also "Grama Vi" to my kids; she was named Viola Mae after her mother, though she never liked the name. And I am a proud Grama Julie to four so far. But now I truly do digress...

Spices (here nutmeg and mace) drying on Pulau Run, Maluku, Indonesia, 2006

For a little taste (!) of more, see Julie Berger Hochstrasser, "The Bones in Banda: Vision, Art, and Memory in Maluku" – online at https://apps.carleton. edu/kettering/hochstrasser/]

Our Lives Since Swarthmore

THE CLASS OF 1976

Everyday Breakfast

Yosef (Jody) Branse

It would be presumptuous to describe this submission as a recipe. In culinary matters I defer to my wife, who is a marvelous cook.

However, on work days I am accustomed to eating breakfast and lunch at my desk, with a simple, quickly-prepared but tasty repast laid out beside my computer. My standard breakfast consists of hummus, cottage cheese and diced yellow pepper on rice cakes.

Several years ago, when the library where I work set up a photographic exhibition on eating at the University, the graphic artist in charge of the project asked to include a shot of my sumptuous breakfast.

Yosef (Jody) Branse and his breakfast at the University of Haifa Library

Tomatoes

Brian Smiga

My grandmother was an illiterate immigrant from Naples, but she managed her property and made the best sauce and bread. You could not visit her without a five-course meal going on the plastic tablecloth in her kitchen. To this day, my siblings and I all raise our own tomatoes, and I believe that we've raised the next gen to garden more productively.

Besides sauce and salads (and I grow all the ingredients that go into each on my Jersey shore ocean cliff plot - Come visit Classmates!), nothing compares to thin sliced tomatoes, mozzarella, basil with garlic or pepper infused oil and balsamic glaze, salt, pepper and turmeric.

Among my favorite places when returning to campus is the kitchen garden outside Sharples.

Dr. Newman's Own Balsamic Vinaigrette

Paul Newman

I got the original recipe from my wife's fellow graduate student at MIT, Claire Welty who is now the director of the Center for Urban Environmental Research and Education at University of Maryland, Baltimore County. The original recipe called for red wine vinegar, but one time I had run out of that and used balsamic vinegar instead – much better! I have attached a photo of a batch I made recently in a salad dressing bottle I bought many years ago. To the right is an old jar in which I store the mix of dry ingredients to save time adding them fresh each time. The jar originally contained artichoke hearts I purchased many years ago. Look closely at the label on top and you will see that the purchase price was $1.09!!

Ingredients

- Combine equal parts dried mustard, paprika, and salt, and store extra in a jar for next time.
- 2 tsp of the above mixture
- ½ tsp freshly ground pepper
- 3 cloves garlic pressed
- 1 part Balsamic Vinegar
- 2-3 parts Extra Virgin Olive Oil
- I use a funnel to add the ingredients into an old salad dressing bottle. You might want to shake before adding the oil; it is harder to get the dry to mix in after the oil is added (or add 1 tsp water to help emulsify the mixture).

Traditional Open Face Danish Sandwiches

Cynthia Rasmussen

Using the Danish bread you baked a few pages back ... Here are some traditional Danish open-faced sandwiches. You may notice that all the sandwich recipes start with butter on the bread. "Smorrebrod", the term for open faced sandwich in Danish comes from "smor og brod," literally "butter and bread." If you've ever tasted real Danish butter, you'd know why!

Smörgåsbord is a type of Scandinavian meal served buffet-style with multiple hot and cold dishes of various foods on a table, the main ingredients of which are bread, butter and cheese. Smörgåsbord became internationally known at the 1939 New York World's Fair when it was offered at the Swedish Pavilion "Three Crowns Restaurant."

Roast beef
Rye bread, butter, lettuce, thinly sliced roast beef, remoulade, grated horse radish, pickled cucumbers, watercress and roasted onions

Egg and shrimp
Rye bread, butter, lettuce, hard-boiled egg, shrimp, mayonnaise, caviar, watercress, a piece of tomato and top it with a slice of lemon

Flæskesteg
Rye bread, butter, lettuce, pork roast, crispy pork crackling, pickled red cabbage, pickled cucumbers, watercress and a slice of orange

Fish filet with shrimp
Rye bread, butter, lettuce, a freshly seared fish filet with a rye coating, remoulade, shrimp, watercress, a piece of tomato and top it with a slice of lemon

Boiled brisket
Rye bread, butter, lettuce, thinly sliced boiled brisket, creamed horse radish, grated horse radish, finely chopped mixed pickle, watercress

Ham
Rye bread, butter, lettuce, thinly sliced ham, scrambled eggs, asparagus, julienne carrots, watercress and a piece of fresh cucumber on the top.

Leverpostej
Rye bread, butter, liver pâté, roasted mushrooms, crispy bacon, pickled beet root

Spiced meat roll
Rye bread, butter, lettuce, thinly sliced spiced meat roll, meat jelly, onions in rings and watercress

The midnight snack
Rye bread, butter, liver pâté, corned beef, meat jelly, onions in rings and watercress

I'm sure you're now inspired to come up with your own combination!

Black Bean Salad – Dawson style

Petrina (Albulescu) Dawson

This is one of my favorite go-to recipes – I invented it when I realized that I had to go to a hockey potluck, had 4 hours till the party, and wanted to have a sugar, flour and wheat free dish that I could eat too.

Later on, I found a couple of recipes for Texas caviar that were very similar.

This recipe is more of a suggestion of potential elements to go in your salad: you can use almost anything you have in your pantry or your refrigerator through trial and error. If you are not sure that the mixture will work, take a small amount of the mixture add a sample of the new ingredient and try it out: if you like it, use it!

Ingredients

- 1 can of black beans, rinsed
- 1 cup hearts of palm chopped up (and/or canned peaches, avocado, diced green peppers)
- 1 cup roasted peppers (and/or cherry tomato halves)
- 1 cup cubed cheese (queso fresco, pepper jack, Monterey jack, asiago, etc.)
- 1 cup diced scallions (only if you like them)
- 1 cup cooked corn cooled (from can or frozen)
- Salt & pepper to taste
- ½ cup of mild or medium salsa or a bit more if it the salsa is chunky and you need to coat the ingredients
- ¼ cup of Italian salad dressing

Directions

- Mix, taste… add a little vinegar or lemon if you like it more acidity…
- Garnish with fresh parsley or cilantro if you have it…
- Refrigerate for a few hours

Jamie Dawson (9 years old)

St. Louis Salad from Patti G.

Carol Swingle

I'll add one of my favorite recipes from the days when I did do some food preparation. There was a restaurant in St. Louis in the 1970's-80's called "Rich and Charlie's." One of their signature dishes was a salad. This is my friend's rendering of the recipe for that salad.

Salad Makings

- 1 head iceberg lettuce (only if the farmworkers weren't on strike!)
- ½ lb spinach
- 1 16-oz can (drained) grapefruit
- 1 avocado, sliced
- ½ cup cashews

Dressing (makes enough for 3 salads)

- ⅔ cup vinegar
- 1½ cups oil
- 2 tsp salt
- 1½ Tbsp celery seed
- ½ cup grated onion
- ⅔ cup sugar
- 2 tsp dry mustard
- Blend ingredients in a blender until of desired consistency.
- Serves 4

Antonio (Nevers) DiMicco's Cheesesteak or Italian Sausage Sandwich

Debbie Vernon DiMicco

The sausage and steak recipes come from 40 years in Seaside Heights NJ and the Allentown Fair in PA. Both recipes are from Bruce's father, whose nickname was Nevers, and the name of the Allentown stand was Antonio's Italian Sausage. In Seaside it was Nevers Steakhouse (where Bruce spent every summer until age 19).

Cheesesteak sandwich

- First, purchase good Italian rolls.
- Preheat rolls at 250°F in the oven.
- Prepare fried peppers and onions prior to steak being cooked, set aside.
- In a frying pan add olive oil, when very hot, add beef steak (chipped steak that you can find in the frozen food meat sections preferably rib eye).
- Place meat in pan and proceed to slice and dice with spatula and knife (shredding the meat). When half done, season the meat with pixie dust. Pixie dust is ⅓ pepper and ⅔ granulated garlic.
- Place sliced cheese over steak, turn heat off top with onions and peppers.

Italian Sausage sandwich

- Add ¼ inch water to an electric skillet, and heat to 400F.
- Place links of Italian sausage (8-12 inches in length) in the skillet, turn every one to two minutes in the boiling water. Continue turning until sausage browns and inside of links are brownish pink. Turn skillet off, slice links into 4-5 inch lengths.
- Place in Italian rolls with fried onions and peppers (which you already did with the cheesesteak). (Add tomato sauce if you choose.)

Thom's Sweet Potato Spinach Pizza

Bruce Robertson

This sounds like an utterly unlikely combination (and I can't say the photo makes it look its best) but it works and it is incredibly simple. And vegan.

We love making pizza, but we are very easy on ourselves — we never make the dough. At a certain point we knew we needed to eliminate cheese from our diets: that old cholesterol problem (and I can tell you that with only that change in diet we cut our scores by nearly 20 points). So Thom, my husband, started fooling around with cheeseless pizza recipes. This is his biggest success and my favorite.

Pizza toppings

- Sweet potatoes and spinach.

Directions

Potatoes

- For the potatoes, peel them, and then take a mandoline slicer and cut very thin slices of potato. Do this first, and let them marinate in olive oil, salt and pepper until you're ready to use them. One thing to learn to live with is that you will always have a big chunk of the sweet potato leftover. You could cut it up into chunks and roast them—but I almost never get around to doing that. I can't think of another use. [Petrina suggests: sweet potato chips!]

Spinach

- For the spinach, wet the spinach and wilt it in a covered pot until it is one green mass at the bottom of the pot, and not burnt (so pay attention to the wilting). Take it out, and on a cutting board, squeeze out excess water and chop into large chunks.

Dough

- The dough: we only ever buy it. Trader Joe's is perfectly good, but we now have found better dough at our high-end local supermarket at their bakery/deli counter. They sell pizza slices but will sell you the dough as well. You can easily find the equivalent.

- We roll it out very thin. The secret to pizza we have discovered—a tip from our Italian neighbor across the street—is to use parchment paper instead of a pizza stone. There are several advantages. The first is I have never succeeded in making a round pizza and pizza stones accommodate round pizzas only. I have learned to live with the result of whatever I manage to roll out: I either make states or islands. Cyprus and Texas are two frequent results. Sometimes I get California too. I never get Montana, the Dakotas or Carolinas, or any straight-edged state.

- The second advantage is that while I roll out the dough first on the wooden pizza shovel—owning one is actually critical, unlike the stupid stone thing—I then transfer it to the parchment paper, where I can roll it in any direction to the thinness I want. The third advantage is you always know when the pizza is done because the two "handles" of paper, the extra edges on either end, turn brown, and then you know it's ready, and you can actually take it out by the paper edges (although I also support it with the pizza shovel). I love parchment paper and now roast every vegetable on it. So easy!

- Do not put a cooking sheet under the paper. It's just the paper in the oven with the pizza on top and the metal below.

- When the dough is rolled out, brush the edges with olive oil (but not the center since the potatoes are oily anyway), and lay out the potato slices all over it. Put it in a 500F oven on a middle shelf until the edges of the crust (and the paper) are brown. Take out and place spinach in small clumps all over it.

- Cut into slices and serve.

- Rorschach test: which state or island is this?

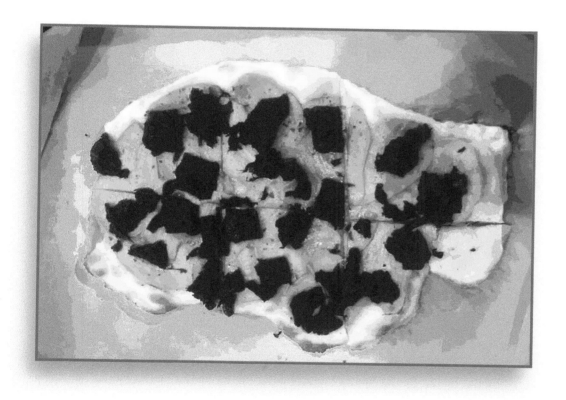

Garbanzo Stew from Todd Speece

Carol Swingle

Ingredients

- 2 Tbsp Olive Oil
- 1 Very Large Onion, coarsely chopped
- 4 cups Carrots, Coarsely Sliced (1/2")
- 4 cloves Chopped Garlic
- 1 Tbsp Smoked Paprika
- 2 tsp Turmeric
- 1 tsp Coarse Ground Black Pepper
- ¼ cup Golden Flaxseed Meal
- 2 cans Garbanzo Beans
- 2 tsp Garlic Bouillon (I Use Better Than Bouillon)
- ¼ cup Flour
- ½ cup Cold Water
- 11 oz Package Fresh Baby Spinach (Or One Pound Fresh)

Directions

- Prepare two cups of your favorite brown rice. While the rice is cooking, prepare the stew.
- In a large stew pot over medium heat, sauté the carrots, garlic & onions in the olive oil for about 5 minutes – until carrots are tender.
- Add the pepper, paprika and turmeric as well as the garlic bouillon and the two cans of undrained garbanzo beans. Continue to cook over medium heat.
- Add the flour to the ½ cup water and mix thoroughly – I use a small Tupperware container as a shaker and mix it vigorously.
- Add the flour mixture to the beans & carrots and continue to cook for 3-5 minutes to create a moderate thickness gravy stirring regularly.
- When you're ready to serve the stew, turn off the heat and add the spinach to the stew mixture. The heat of the stew will wilt the spinach.
- Serve over the brown rice.

Amatriciana alla Steinbrook

Tom Drescher

I offer this recipe in memory of my Swarthmore advisor and friend, the late David Steinbrook (1941-2002), who first cooked this dish for me and my wife in 1995 during a short visit to the temporary apartment in Burbank, CA., where I had relocated to work on the Sam Raimi film, "The Quick and the Dead." David was living in the Bay Area at the time, had remarried, and was busy redecorating his house. We hadn't seen each other in a couple years, and his local Ikea was out of some of the cabinets he wanted for his kitchen, so one weekend he decided to drive down to LA for a visit, and to get those "Knoxhult" pieces he wanted at the Ikea branch down the street. On the way back, we stopped along Magnolia Blvd. at the Italian import store so David could grab some pancetta and a couple cans of good Italian tomatoes to make Amatriciana for the four of us. He was a good cook, and liked the dish pretty spicy. It was fantastic. High class comfort food if ever there was any, even in hot weather. David, I miss you.

Note: Many recipes for this dish add a couple cloves of garlic, but it's not traditional. Also, this amount of sauce would usually make enough for 4 servings, but twice as much is twice as nice in my book. Prep time, about 40 min. Serves 2.

Ingredients

- 3 Tbsp olive oil
- 1 medium yellow onion, peeled and chopped
- 1-28 oz can San Marzano imported Italian whole peeled tomatoes
- 4 oz pancetta (or unsmoked bacon)
- ½ tsp red pepper flakes
- ¾ cup freshly grated parmesan cheese
- 6 oz. spaghetti (I use whole wheat – imported from Italy is best)

Our wedding: Top row: Myself, Andrea Brown, David Steinbrook, Ken Moskowitz. Bottom row: Bill Parker, May Zia, Paul Edelman (1982)

Directions

- In a 10" sauté pan, heat the oil and cook the chopped onion over medium heat for 5-6 minutes until it softens and turns golden. Coarsely chunk the tomatoes (easily done while still in the can) and add them to the pan, removing any basil leaves. Mix in the red pepper flakes. Turn the heat down to low and simmer uncovered for about 20 minutes until the sauce has thickened, stirring occasionally to prevent sticking.

- While the sauce is reducing, bring a pot of water to a boil for the pasta. Cut the pancetta into smallish pieces, and cook them in a separate pan until medium crispy, draining most of the fat. When the sauce is about 10 minutes from being done, mix in the pancetta.

- Cook and drain the pasta. Add the pasta to the saucepan, turn the heat to low and marry it all together for a few minutes, stirring constantly. Mix in the grated parmesan and toss well before serving. Garnish with additional parmesan if you desire (which you do, right?)

- This dish is best accompanied by a small salad, and a light, very dry red wine – Grenache, Malbec, Chianti, or a nice Nebbiolo.

Spaghetti Carbonara

Liz Loeb McCane

When Jim and I moved onto our sailboat in 1979, we knew meal planning would be a challenge. Our boat lacked refrigeration and an oven, so we did all of our cooking on a two-burner kerosene stove – for six years!

Early in our travels we bought a cookbook entitled The Cruising Chef (Mike Greenwald, Tab Books, 1977) which gave us many ideas for meals from a limited kitchen.

To this day, our favorite recipe is Spaghetti Carbonara; I've ordered it in restaurants but it's never as good as this recipe.

Did you know that bacon comes in cans, and that eggs and parmesan cheese don't have to be refrigerated?

We always had everything needed for this meal!

Ingredients

- Hot spaghetti
- Bacon and grease
- ¼ cup olive oil
- 3 egg yolks, well beaten
- 1 cup grated Parmesan cheese (the real thing!)
- 6 cloves chopped garlic

Directions

- Fry 1 lb bacon, cut into 1" pieces. Boil and drain 1 lb spaghetti
- Mix thoroughly, add salt to taste. Serves 4 people.
- My modifications: I add the minced garlic to bacon very briefly at the very end of frying. I use 2 whole eggs instead of yolks. I mix the beaten eggs with Parmesan before adding to pasta.

On Meatloaf

Linda Grimaldi

I am an omnivore. I revel in the fact. Not only can I eat almost every kind of food there is, I enjoy almost every kind of food there is. There are people who have eliminated entire classes of food from their diets out of health concerns, necessity, taste, or a specific sense of ethics. I am not among them. But I digress.

For now, I sing of meatloaf. I first learned to make meatloaf by watching my mother. She made a great meatloaf. She could carry on an in-depth conversation while her hands decided the mixture didn't have the right feel- needed water, more breadcrumb, something. She would make the correction and keep talking. Hers always had a strip of bacon on top and was always delicious.

However, my mother and I are different kinds of cooks. She was remarkably consistent and stuck to a fairly predictable repertoire of dishes. Me, well, consistency never was my strong point. Even if I have never cooked a particular dish before, my approach is not to cook from a recipe but to read every recipe I can find for something- cassoulet or aloo gobi, whatever – and wing it from there. It generally works. And if it doesn't, we are privileged enough that an occasional dinner of cereal and milk is considered "brinner", not a hardship. Hard to believe I was a chemistry major...

As I made my way in the world, I discovered people did all sorts of things with meatloaf. They put crushed cornflakes in instead of breadcrumbs. They used different spices. They left out the cheese. They even wrapped the meat mixture around things like whole carrots and hardboiled eggs. I recognized meatloaf as quite conducive to my cooking style- a comfortable theme with limitless variations that make it an omnivore's delight and give you the opportunity to clean out the fridge.

The odd droopy leaf of kale or chard, the zucchini in the back of the fridge that really has to get used, left over winter squash puree or beans or canned tomatoes- all misfit vegetables are candidates for throwing in the mix. Cereal can work as filler, but I prefer breadcrumbs, soaked bulgur or leftover steel cut oats. The choice really affects texture.

As far as the meat goes, the source doesn't matter as long as you pay attention to the ratio of fat to lean (two thirds lean beef, one third pork generally works) and, if you use poultry, throw in some roasted mushrooms to up the umami.

To accommodate the less omnivorous, while I wouldn't call it meatloaf (almonds don't produce milk, either), lentils, cheese, quinoa and olive oil can work as well. Season according to mood- anything from our family classic basil-garlic-parmesan to five spice powder.

I can't provide a recipe, but here are some rough rules of thumb:

- About a third as much dry breadcrumb or other filler as meat by volume- adjust if the filler is pre-soaked.

- About a quarter as much grated Parmesan as meat by volume if you want an Italian touch One egg per pound of meat.

- Some veggies, chopped finely if you want a consistent texture. Minced onions add nice flavor and copious quantities of parsley are rarely a mistake.

- A little liquid- water, wine, stock, canned tomato, soya sauce, etc. - just to make sure things aren't too dry. You'll have to gauge by feel, particularly depending on the other ingredients used. A mix with more veggies generally requires less liquid.

- Preferred spice profile. For us, Italian is traditional. Sometimes I'll do a lamb loaf with Arabic spices, or poultry mix with some dill or just throw in ginger, garlic and chopped chiles.

- As an extra, place a thin layer of chopped root vegetables around the meatloaf as it cooks. Not too many – a thick layer will steam rather than roast and add too much water to the cooking environment.

- Before committing to the oven, take a little piece of the mixture, pan-fry it and taste. Refine and repeat.

Just remembered... have some leftover Chinese pork dumpling filling in the freezer. I think I feel a meatloaf coming on.

Salmon Pie

Deb von Roeder

Although some of you may remember our ice cream trips to the Village Porch or my passing around bowls of chocolate chip cookie dough in a psych lecture, what I'll submit here is an easy savory dish I call "salmon pie."

With a salad and glass of wine, it's an easy go-to meal. And if you don't want the pastry (or to prep it), it's good without too.

Ingredients

- 2 beaten eggs
- ½ cup milk
- 1 Tbsp butter, melted
- ¼ cup chopped onion
- 2 Tbsp minced parsley
- ¾ tsp basil
- ¼ tsp salt
- Either 1 lb can (2 cups) salmon or six 5-7 oz cans tuna
- Pastry for one 8" round (See Debbie DiMicco's crust recipe in Family Apple Pie or just buy a pre-made crust)

Directions

- Combine eggs, milk, butter, onion, parsley, & seasonings. Break salmon in chunks, removing bones & skin. Stir salmon into egg mixture. Pour into well-greased 8" pie plate.
- Prepare pastry, mix & roll 1/8" onto the top in wedges.
- Bake at 425F approx. 25 mins. Serve with chilled cucumber sauce:

Sauce

- 1 med. cucumber
- 1 Tbsp minced parsley
- 1 tbsp grated onion
- ¼ cup mayonnaise
- 2 tsp vinegar
- ½ cup sour cream
- salt & pepper
- Cut cucumber in half lengthwise and scoop out seeds. Grate to make 1 cup. Drain well. Blend all & chill. Makes approx. 1½ cups of sauce.

Deb von Roeder and Lise Weisberger

Cottage Pie

Ian Chitty

We have been living in Bawtry for the last 33 years – and we are only some 25 miles from the centre of Sheffield, and while Bawtry was a port on the River Idle in 12th Century- it wouldn't have taken anything with a draft of more than about 3 feet, and the river has long since silted to the point where it is now not navigable. I live in Bawtry, but Austerfield, which is little more than a mile from Bawtry, is part of the Parish of which I am a member of the joint Parochial Church Council (PCC) covering the totality of both.

As to a typical local dish – I guess Yorkshire Pudding would be the most obvious answer- though of course it's not a pudding – but a batter accompaniment to roast beef and gravy. The other typical dish would be cottage or shepherds pie – which while this sounds boring, but can be made to taste fabulous if cooked my way.

Ingredients

- 1lb-11 oz/750g of minced low-fat beef (alternatively lamb for Shepherd's pie)
- 2 or 3 apple size onions
- 3 or 4 x 6 in carrots
- Enough potatoes to make into mashed potato to cover the whole dish to a depth of approx. 1 in.
- Dried mixed herbs – liberal sprinkling
- Salt and black pepper seasoning
- Beef gravy granules/ Oxo cubes
- HP Sauce- or similar BBQ sauce if preferred
- A knob of butter
- ¼ Pt milk

The Mayflower Pub, less than 100 yards from the church

Directions

- Slice and dice the onions having peeled the outer skins. Melt butter or use olive oil in frying pan (skillet) and brown turning frequently to reduce.

- Peel your potatoes and place in saucepan of boiling water for around 10 mins. Test that potatoes are ready for mashing by sticking the point of a knife into several and see if they slide off. Peel carrots and slice into little wheels.

- Once the onions have partially browned, add the minced beef to the onions in the frying pan/skillet. Mix the onions in with the beef and keep turning the beef and onions until all the beef turns from red through to grey, then to deep brown, indicating that it is fried.

- Add mixed herbs, crushed Oxo cubes (2 or 3), add gravy powder liberally and stir in. Add quarter of pint of water and stir in so the gravy browning forms a sauce with herbs.

St. Helena Austerfield, Yorkshire (where William Bradford, first governor of Massachusetts, was baptized)

- Take an oven safe dish, approx. 3 ins deep and tip the entire contents of the frying pan into it. Add your sliced carrots and mix in evenly.

- Mash your potatoes adding butter, plus a little milk and salt and pepper. Make this slightly drier than you would normally if you were serving Mashed Potato as a separate dish.

- Take the mashed potato and using a flat kitchen utensil, spread the mashed potato evenly to a depth of about 1 inch across the entire top of the oven dish. Then take a fork and scour the surface of the potatoes so that it looks as if you have a miniature ploughed field – but making sure that at no point any of the furrows penetrate to the meat and gravy below.

- Place the Cottage pie at the top of a preheated oven at around 230c (450F) for approx. 35 mins- or until you can see the top of the furrows beginning to brown.

Madelyn's Dry Cured Salmon with Skordalia Sauce

Madelyn Wessel

Pacific Northwest indigenous peoples have retained fishing rights to the Columbia River salmon. During salmon runs, you can drive out the Columbia Gorge from Portland and buy a fresh whole salmon from the tribes. The taste of one of these wild fish, rubbed in herbs and salt, wrapped in tin foil, and slow roasted over a fire while the fat drips out causing minor explosions, is unbelievable.

This recipe has been refined to produce something of the same taste and texture. Interestingly, you need to use Atlantic salmon (farm raised is fine) for the recipe to work out best given the curing process.

Ingredients

- 3 pounds of Atlantic salmon, skin on. (Probably two whole sides, depending on size of fish.) Go with more, rather than less. Fish is delicious cold and reheated.

Dry rub mix:

- ½ cup coarse sea salt
- 1 cup brown sugar
- 3 bay leaves, crumbled/torn
- 1 tsp black peppercorns
- ½ tsp garlic powder
- ½ tsp garam masala (Indian spice, at Whole Foods and Foods of All Nations)
- ½ tsp dried red pepper flakes
- 1 tsp dried rosemary

Directions

- At about 1 PM on the day of the dinner, thickly coat the fish on both sides with the rub. Place the fish skin side up (flesh side down) in a long Pyrex or other non-reactive pan. Cover with plastic and put into the refrigerator for about five hours. When you return, you will find the fish has drained a lot of fluid. This is good!
- Rinse the fish carefully and quickly in cold water. Dry with paper towels and put skin side down, (flesh side up) on a large cookie sheet lined with parchment paper. Paint the roasting glaze (below) on the fish and cover again with plastic wrap. Refrigerate until ready for dinner.

Roasting glaze:

- 2 Tbsp black bean garlic sauce
- 2 Tbsp lemon juice
- 2 Tbsp olive oil
- 1 tsp honey
- Mix together and glaze the fish.
- Every oven is different, so: Roast the fish in a 400F for about 12-15 minutes. Check the fish to see that it has browned very slightly on top and is cooked through but not dry. If fish is underdone, add a few minutes. If fish is not browning slightly throw on the broiler for 30

seconds. (If you like the recipe, try grilling outside sometime in good weather. I grill the fish all year long on top of dried rosemary branches harvested from my garden.)

- Surround the fish with lemon slices and serve immediately.

Skordalia Sauce:
(Please forgive fact that all proportions are guesstimates; however, this sauce is very forgiving of experimentation!)

In a food processor, first grind up together:

- 4-5 cloves of garlic (depending on size)

- 2-3 shallots (depends on size)

- 1 heaping Tbsp capers

- Add and grind up: 1 big bunch each of roughly chopped Italian parsley and cilantro. (If you are buying wimpy little bunches at your grocer then use two.)

- After that is chopped, add: 2/3 cup of almonds (ideal if you have some around, or pecans or walnuts if you don't)

Now add:

- Several small pieces of white bread (baguette, sourdough, whatever you have) soaked in cold water and gently squeezed

- ½ cup cold water

- Juice from two good lemons

- 1 tsp sea salt

- A robust amount of fresh ground black pepper

- Some red pepper flakes

- And then while your processor is running slowly pour in about a cup of olive oil (More may be needed. To be honest, I never measure this. I just pour from the bottle until the sauce looks right.)

- This should be turning into a thick, rich, bright green sauce. Now it's time to taste it and add what you want: A bit more water if the sauce is too thick. More salt/pepper/ red pepper flakes. If the sauce is too tart add a bit more olive oil.

In the summer when I have fresh herbs I will throw in a few leaves of lemon balm or pineapple sage. Do NOT use basil! It turns brown and is not good in this sauce. Skordalia keeps well in the fridge.

Sunday Dinner at the Gibbs House

Derrick Gibbs

I've enjoyed cooking since my Swarthmore days. I remember trying to make pepper steak on those crummy hot plates in the dorm.

Fast forward 40+ years, I'm not a foodie, but I like eating and making specialty dishes. This is a photo of Sunday dinner I made for my wife. A good time was had by all!

Clockwise from bottom right: Cranberry Barbecue Chicken, Brown Rice, Collard Greens, Curry Peas and Rice. Center: Jerk Salmon

Cranberry Barbecue Chicken
(Adaptable for cooking on a stove or outdoor cooking)

On the Stove

- Mince onion, garlic and green peppers.

- Prepare chicken by washing and cutting to your desired size.

- Sautée all ingredients in your favorite oil in a frying pan (iron skillet preferred) for approx. 10 minutes.

- Open a can of cranberries (whole berries) and mix it with your favorite barbecue sauce in the proportion of 1/4 cranberries to 3/4 barbecue.

- Add a dash of your mustard of choice (I use Grey Poupon) and a dash of cayenne (optional).

- Pour sauce on the chicken into the pan and cook on a low heat. Finish cooking on the stove top or place the iron skillet in the oven and bake at 400 degrees. Turn chicken periodically until chicken is cooked. If the sauce gets more dry than desired, add a little chicken stock.

Outdoor Cooking

Make sauce as stated above and apply to the chicken. Use your preferred method for cooking the chicken – grilling, barbecuing, or smoking. Apply additional sauce periodically.

Jerk Salmon

(Adaptable for cooking in an oven or outdoor cooking)

On the Stove

- Measure ½ cup of mayonnaise.
- Add 2 table spoons of jerk sauce (I use Walker's Wood Traditional Jerk Sauce) –your choice of mild or hot. If jerk sauce is too hot for you, substitute mustard as a great alternative to jerk sauce. Stir the mixture and sprinkle in a teaspoon of garlic powder.
- Prepare salmon (fillets or steaks) by washing and pat dry.
- Apply the marinade to the top side of the salmon and let sit for 20 minutes (unless you're in a hurry, then you can put it directly in the oven at 400 degrees. Apply additional thin layer of marinade after 10 minutes and continue cooking for another 10 minutes or until done to your satisfaction.

Outdoor Cooking

- Make marinade as stated above, then apply it to the top side of the salmon. Let marinade sit for 20 minutes (unless you're in a hurry). Use your preferred method for cooking the salmon – grilling, barbecuing, or smoking.
- Apply additional marinade per your preference.

Fiesta Shrimp

It's Tuesday night and my wife and I collaborated on a 15 minute meal. Quick can be tasty. Then we have plenty of time to watch "This is Us" or MSNBC.

- Drizzle sesame oil in a frying pan sauté onions, red peppers and carrots toss in the shrimp and cilantro
- Salt and pepper to taste.
- Bonus: If you want a little extra zing, add pesto sauce.

Gege's Fish Papillotes

Gina Doggett

The quantities here are approximate, as my husband never measures. And the possible variations are myriad, often simply depending on the ingredients on hand. But here is a basic recipe for a meal that is always a hit, coming in a tidy little package on the plate, to open like a present, letting lovely scented steam escape to reveal a fish smothered in healthy veggies and heavenly herbs.

The main course is all in the bundle, kept warm by its wrapping. Dinner for four to enjoy with bread and white wine!

Ingredients

- 4 small fillets of whiting, cod or salmon
- 2 finely chopped shallots
- 1 leek, julienned
- Red bell pepper, chopped into small pieces
- Optional sliced mushrooms, diced tomatoes
- Optional ginger, preferably fresh, diced tout petit petit
- Also cumin, lemon grass, rosemary, thyme, bay leaf -- to taste
- A handful of flat-leaf parsley, chopped
- Splashes of dry white wine
- Lemon slices
- Salt and pepper

Directions

- Preheat oven to 400F.
- Use rectangles of aluminum foil around 10 by 5 inches, anticipating that they must enclose the fish and veg, then be sealed tight.
- Lay down the leeks, shallots and parsley first, add the fish, then top with the mushrooms and lemon slices. Add a splash of white wine and salt and pepper.
- Create the foil packages, starting at the ends, then the sides, folding the foil over itself along the top, making sure the papillotes are airtight to seal in all that goodness.
- Stick them in the oven for 20 minutes or so. Open yours to check for doneness.
- Et voila!

Danish Donuts (Aebleskiver)

Cynthia Rasmussen

Aebleskiver is the traditional spherical Danish pancake, resembling a large donut hole, eaten with Glogg (mulled wine, see recipe) at Advent or for a sweet treat. They are made in a special cast-iron half ball pan, and can be served with syrup, jam, or powdered sugar. They can also be filled during the cooking process with jelly, chocolate chips, nut butter, or applesauce. Although this family recipe does not call for it, I will often add a pinch of cardamom or cinnamon to the batter.

Turning the aebleskiver to cook the second side is traditionally done with a knitting needle or a pointed chopstick (see online YouTube videos), but I find it easiest to use a fork, snag one cooked edge of the pastry with one of the tines, and pull it up and over to the opposite side of the hemispherical depression in the pan, depositing the uncooked batter into the well, and forming a roof with the cooked half. It can be messy until you get the hang of it, but that's half the fun.

Ingredients

- 3 eggs, separated, with whites beaten to soft peaks
- 2 cups buttermilk
- 2 cups sifted flour
- 1 tsp baking soda
- 2 Tbsp sugar
- ¼ cup melted butter
- ½ tsp salt

Directions

- In a bowl, beat the egg yolks until thick and lemon colored; gradually beat in the sugar. Add the combined buttermilk and melted butter alternately with the mixed and sifted flour, soda, and salt. Gently fold in the beaten egg whites.
- In a heated cast iron half-ball pan, drop in a bit of butter so as to grease the pan. Pour in the batter, filling the wells 2/3 full. Cook until bubbles appear and break around the edges of each half-ball of batter. Turn and cook on the other side for about 2 minutes. Total cooking time per batch around 5 minutes.
- Remove each ball and roll in confectioners' sugar (I place ½ cup of confectioners' sugar in a paper bag and shake the freshly cooked donuts to coat them). Repeat the procedure until all the batter is used.
- Keep warm and serve as a dessert or breakfast with syrup, jam, or jelly.
- If a half-ball pan is not available, this batter may be cooked as a dessert pancake (you could use metal rings on the griddle for a hockey puck approximation of the round aebleskiver also). If you are going to fill them, add the filling to the center of the batter just after pouring the batter into the wells and press the filling down into the batter so they flip without leaking.

Macarons and Walnut Bread

Pamela Casper

I lived in Paris for two years directly after Swarthmore, it was the perfect antidote to four years of Swarthmore food. Here are two recipes from my favorite books.

Macarons au Chocolat (Chocolate Macaroons)
(Recipe from *French Tea: The Pleasures of the Table* by Carol Manchester)

The Macaron: now you can make them yourself! I first ate a macaron in 1976 made in the bakery across from my Paris studio apartment. Biting into one of those for the first time I thought, it was heaven on earth! When I returned to NY in 1979 I thought about bringing them to NY when I worked as the pastry buyer at Dean and Deluca. What I should have done was go into business with them alone. Just look now at the macaron craze in NYC and across America. A missed opportunity.

From Carol Manchester, *French Tea: The Pleasures of the Table*

Ingredients for the cookie:

- 3 large egg whites
- ½ cup granulated sugar
- 1⅓ cups confectioner's sugar
- ⅓ cup cocoa powder
- ¾ cup finely ground blanched almonds

Directions for the cookies:

- Preheat the oven to 300°F. Line several baking sheets with parchment paper.
- In a bowl, using an electric mixer, beat the egg white until they hold soft peaks. Gradually add the sugar, and beat until the whites form stiff peaks.
- Sift the confectioner's sugar, cocoa powder, and almonds together. Gently but thoroughly fold the almond mixture into the whites in 2 or 3 additions. Transfer the mixture to a pastry bag fitted with a decorative tip. Pipe the mixture onto the prepared baking sheets, forming 1-inch high mounds about 2 inches apart. Use a spatula to smooth the tops of the macaroons. Bake for 15-18 minutes, or until the tops of the macaroons are firm. Let cool completely. Remove the macaroons from the parchment paper, and store in an airtight tin for 1 week.

Ingredients for the filling:

- ½ pint raspberries
- ¼ cup heavy cream
- 8 oz bittersweet chocolate
- 2 Tbsp unsalted butter, softened
- 1 Tbsp eau de vie des franboises

Directions for the filling:

- In a small saucepan, combine the raspberries and cream. Cook over moderate heat, stirring and mashing the berries into the cream for 5 minutes or until thickened. Meanwhile, in the top of a double boiler set over simmering water, melt the chocolate.
- Add the butter and raspberry liqueur to the melted chocolate and stir until smooth. Add the raspberry mixture and stir until well combined. Transfer to a bowl, cover, and chill until set.

To form the cookies:

- Using a small knife, smooth a thin layer of the chocolate filling on the bottom of a macaroon. Top with another macaroon to form a sandwich. Repeat with the remaining macaroons and filling. Transfer to airtight containers, separating each layer of cookies with waxed paper. Cover and refrigerate. Makes about 40 cookies.

Pain aux Noix (Walnut Bread)

Bread is the staple of life and here is one of my favorites. (Recipe from *The Breads of France* by Bernard Clayton, Jr.)

Ingredients

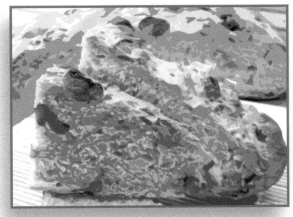

From Bernard Clayton Jr., *The Breads of France*

- 3¾ cups whole wheat flour
- 1 cup all-purpose flour
- 2 cups lukewarm water
- 1 Tbsp honey
- 1 cake fresh yeast OR 1 pkg dry yeast
- 2½ tsp salt
- 1¼ cups walnut halves, broken in half
- 1 egg, beaten with ½ tsp salt (for glaze)

Directions

- Put both types of flour in a bowl, make a well in the centre, and pour in a quarter of the water. Add the honey; then crumble the yeast over the ingredients in the well and stir to dissolve. Add the remaining water and the salt and stir gently, gradually drawing in the flour to make a smooth dough. Add more flour if necessary to make a dough that is soft and slightly sticky. Turn the dough out onto a floured board and knead it for 5-10 minutes or until smooth and elastic, adding more flour if it sticks to the board. Put the dough in a lightly oiled bowl, turn it over so the top is oiled and cover with a damp cloth. Leave to rise in a warm place for 1-1½ hours or until doubled in bulk. Butter two 7-inch round cake pans.
- Knead the risen dough lightly to knock out the air, then knead in the walnuts. Shape the dough into 2 round loaves on a floured board. Set them in the pans, cover with a damp cloth, and leave to rise again in a warm place for 30 minutes or until the dough has doubled in size. Meanwhile, set the oven at 425°F.
- Before baking, slash the top of each love 3 or 4 times with a knife and brush with egg glaze. Bake for 15 minutes or until the loaves begin to brown. Lower the heat to 375°F and continue baking for another 30-40 minutes, or until the loaves sound hollow when tapped on the bottom.

Heidi's Bread

Julie Berger Hochstrasser

In loving memory of Heidi Lieben Hochstrasser

(March 21, 1987- December 4, 2016)

Which of my daughter's recipes to share with you? I just happen to have this one here, written in her own hand, so it won. (And it's a good one!) But out in Idaho there's a whole binder full, and then it would have been too tough to choose: croissants or canalés? Or (her favorite) Kouign Amans? Pie filling made with Kabocha squash? Heidi was fearless.

After college she got a job making pies for Companion Bakery in Santa Cruz, California, producing a few pies a week. Soon it was a dozen, then more, and she became their official "pie wench," heading up "Team Butter" in charge of pastry while her friend managed "Team Crust" for the bread. She even produced all the pies for the famous Pie Ranch in Pescadero.

She sweetly claimed I taught her everything she knew, but that was so not true—I couldn't have begun to guess how much flour to order every week for an entire bakery, or how to run a stand mixer the size of a small Volkswagen.

But Heidi was fearless not only in the kitchen.

She had studied abroad in Concepcion, Chile, and after we met her at Macchu Picchu, continued to trek around Patagonia. She built her own bike and rode it from Barcelona to Paris, stopping at bakeries all along the way "in search of the perfect croissant."

When she and her boyfriend moved to Driggs, Idaho, they built the Teton Rock Gym, and she ran their summer camp, and their climbing team, and their after school program, and volunteered cooking lunch for seniors at the community center, and at the CSA at Cosmic Apple Farm....so much of which I only learned from all the deeply grateful parents and others who crowded in to grieve with us after she was suddenly, out of nowhere, killed in an icy collision in a white-out blizzard, coming home from cross-country skiing.

The irony. How we worried every day about a climbing accident, and instead it was this utterly random thing that took her. Now, five years out from that unthinkable day, my husband and I strive to focus on all the wonderful memories, and how blessed we were to have had her in our lives at all.

And she is still so very much with us: every pie I bake, every small triumph in the kitchen, every sumptuous new bakery we relish (not to mention every adventure we enjoy in nature), the spirit of Heidi is right there.

Ingredients

- 3 cups flour (up to half being whole wheat or other)
- 1 to 2 tsp salt
- ¼ tsp yeast
- 1⅝ cups water
- Put in bowl and mix up. Should be "shaggy-sticky."
- Add 2 Tbsp herbs at this point IF you want 'em.

Directions

- Cover tightly with plastic; let sit 12-18 hours.
- Flour a surface and, with a rubber spatula, scrape dough ball out onto surface. Sprinkle with flour, fold over on itself one or two times.
- Cover loosely with plastic; let sit 15 minutes.
- GENEROUSLY flour a towel (smooth cotton—not terry-cloth) laid flat. With lightly floured hands, quickly and gently shape dough into a ball. Place seam-side down. Flour dough lightly, cover with another towel. Let sit two hours.
- Preheat oven to 450° F. Place heavy pot (cast iron, ceramic, etc.) with lid in oven for 20 minutes.
- When pot is hot, slide hand under bottom towel and flip dough ball into pot.
- Dough's seam side will now be up. (Be careful not to let dough stick to towel...if you can!)
- Bake with lid ON at 450° for about 30 minutes.
- Remove lid, bake 15-30 minutes more until crusty and golden brown. Remove from pot.
- Yield: 1½ pound loaf

Heidi with her boyfriend Jacob filling profiteroles

Biscones (Biscuit-Scone)

Gilda Kramer

During COVID-19 lockdown when we could not go out to eat and it was harder to source specialty cooked foods that we enjoyed, I spent a lot of time cooking and baking, often with new recipes. Last summer while visiting our older son prepared "high tea" including delicious scones. I asked him for the recipe, but when I tried it, something wasn't right and they were dry. The next time I made them, I modified the recipe and the result was not quite a scone, and not quite a biscuit, but it was delicious.

Ingredients

- 2 cups sifted all-purpose flour
- 1 Tbsp baking powder
- 2 Tbsp sugar
- ½ tsp salt
- ½ cup butter
- 2 eggs
- ¾ cups creme fraiche
- Optional: fresh blueberries

Directions

- Preheat the oven to 400F. Sift dry ingredients together. Cut the butter into the dry ingredients in a food processor until the mixture crumbles (pulse). Place in a large bowl and make a hollow in the center.

- Save one egg white to brush on top. Beat remaining eggs and combine with the creme fraiche, and then add all at once to the flour mixture and stir. If you want to add fresh blueberries, add them at this point, crushing them lightly to let the juices out. Turn onto a floured board and knead very lightly (a few times only). Divide into two. Make two rounds about 1 inch thick. Cut into 4 wedges. Transfer to a baking sheet with parchment paper. Brush with egg whites and sprinkle with a little sugar.

- Bake for about 15 minutes. Serve with your choice of jam or lemon curd, or just eat them while warm. They also freeze very well.

- Note: If you reduce the butter to 3 Tbsp and the creme fraiche to 1/2 cup they will taste closer to scones and they will still be wonderful!

Romanian Holiday Babka (Cozonac)

Petrina (Albulescu) Dawson

I decided to include this recipe in our reunion cookbook because this is a quintessential Romanian celebration dessert: Christmas, Easter, birthday, wedding, baptism, remembering the dead, praying for the living, harvest day, etc. etc. If it's a special occasion, you get Cozonac!

As I worked at perfecting it, I found that many cultures have similar confections for celebrations or special holidays: Pan de Muerto, Pan Dolce, Mallorcas, Kutchen, King Cake, Kulich, Panettone -- a sweet brioche by any other name has never tasted so good! My grandmother used to make it by hand, with no mixer, no dough hook, kneading the dough for about one hour till the gluten developed.

The recipe is a little more complicated than most, but perseverance pays off! It keeps well in the freezer for months, can be refreshed by the slice in 15 seconds in the microwave, or toasted to perfection. (If it does not work the first couple of times you make it, keep trying, they will get better... bad babkas make great bread pudding).

Ingredients-all at room temperature and the lore is that you need to avoid all drafts!

Dough 1

- 500g flour - 00 very refined pizza flour (Anna Napoletana) or bread flour (AP flour will work also but I strongly suggest that you use the refined pizza flour)
- 300ml of warm milk (will need the extra 50ml of milk if you use the bread or the AP flour)
- 30g fresh yeast or 10g instant dry yeast

Dough 2

- 6 yolks + 1 whole egg
- 150g sugar
- 50ml rum or brandy
- 8-10g of salt (about 1.5% of the flour)
- 200g flour
- 1 scraped vanilla bean or 2 tsp extract
- Zest from one lemon
- 120g unsalted butter (80% fat if possible)

Filling

- 400g ground walnuts
- 200g sugar
- 5 egg whites
- 1 tsp vanilla extract
- 1 tsp orange peel (optional)
- OR 600g-800g of turkish delight diced, or about 1-½ cups of raisins or other dried fruit/candy filling (see below)

For egg wash

- 1 egg yolk with a little milk

Directions for the dough

To create the long and elastic fibers of gluten that will yield puffy light dough you need to let the yeast work without the sugar, egg and butter so you make Dough 1 and you let it autolyse without the egg and butter interfering with the yeast.

Dough 1

- Heat the milk slightly (35 seconds in the microwave to no more than 100F). Place in mixer bowl, add flour (sifted) and yeast and mix with the dough hook at lowest speed. You will get a fairly stiff dough. If it is too stiff (climbs up the hook too much), add another 50ml of milk. Cover bowl with a plastic bag and let rest for 30-45 minutes.

Dough 2

- Make a brown butter (melt butter in a pan while stirring till amber brown) and cool. In a medium bowl add 6 yolks and a whole egg, sugar, salt, vanilla, lemon peel and the rum or brandy (needed to make the dough puffier). Mix and add the brown butter to yield a sweet and salty mayonnaise. Add the 200g of flour, mix, cover with a plastic bag and let it rest for at least 15 minutes.

Final Dough

- After the rest period mix Dough 1 with Dough 2 with the hook at the lowest speed. You may need to stop the mixer and scrape the bottom and sides to make sure the two doughs get mixed. After the dough homogenizes, knead the dough with the hook as follows: 10 minutes of kneading, 10 minutes of rest and 10 minutes of kneading. Perform the windowpane test (see below) and if you don't have a smooth dough, let it rest another 10 minutes and knead another 10 (I usually knead it for 3 sets of 10 minutes).

- Knead until the dough passes the windowpane test (stretch out a small piece of dough with your hand in the form of a translucent rectangle through which you can see, and the dough does not break). In addition, the dough is smooth, elastic, and does not stick to the sides of the bowl, slightly tense but soft. Place in an oiled bowl or plastic container and cover to prove. You can also weigh the dough at this time (approximately 1500 g of dough). Note: if you are adding dry fillings you can add them and mix them in with the dough hook in the last 5 minutes of kneading, or you can add them after the bulk rise.

Bulk Rise

- The bulk rise takes around 3 to 4 hours at 75F room temperature (try not to go over 85F degrees ambient temperature). It can take longer, so wait for the dough to triple in volume. If you need time you can leave the dough in the refrigerator for about 8 -12 hours (overnight) and then take it out next morning and continue the bulk rise till triple in volume. If when you poke the dough the finger indentations remain, then the dough has risen well, if it springs back, let it prove some more. (I usually let mine quadruple)

- Divide the dough depending on your baking pans. If you have 2lb loaves, then you can make two loaves of 750g each and each braid at 375 (2braids). For 1lb (4x9 loaf pans), I divide the dough into 3 parts, 500g each, with each braid at 250 g. I generally weigh each braid and roll it out separately. If you become addicted to brioche breads, I suggest you purchase some heavy-duty pans from USA Pan with straight edges and ridges and your breads will improve!

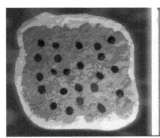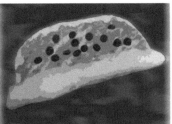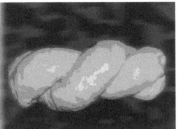

Fillings

- The traditional filling is a nut filling: Roast the walnuts for 7-8 minutes, chop in the food processor on pulse so some bigger pieces remain. Whip the egg whites and the sugar to a soft meringue, add the vanilla and then mix in the walnuts. You can add cinnamon or nutmeg to taste. I have sprinkled chocolate chips on top of the mixture as I make the roll too. (Any filling that remains after making the babka I pipe as meringue kisses and bake at 320 degrees for about 40 minutes...delicious gluten free cookies!)

Other fillings

- You can use your imagination for the fillings, but nothing runny or wet. Other traditional Romanian fillings are diced Turkish delight (you can find on Amazon for about the same price as fruit jelly candy or make your own) or raisins (soaked in rum). Any of chopped dried apricots, dried figs, candied strawberries, candied ginger, craisins, currants, chocolate chips, jellybeans, citron, or the fruit jelly candy that can be cut up (bulk foods in the supermarket). If you use any mixture of these, you can also add to the dough in the last 5 minutes of kneading before the bulk rise (use around 600 g of filling).

Shaping the Babkas

- Oil your pans and put parchment paper along the long sides and re-spray – Pam or equivalent is fine.
- On an oiled surface and with oiled hands, spread out the dough for each braid in a rectangle (either with a rolling pin or with your hands-- I always do it with my hands). Dough should be about 3/8in thick, but does not need to be very uniform – the dough wants to spring back so make sure you stretch it and let it rest till your rectangle does not shrink – the thinner it is the nicer your inner swirls of filling.
- Spread ¼ in thick coating of the walnut filling on the dough leaving about ½ inch at the top without filling, sprinkle some semi-sweet chocolate chips and roll from the bottom, tightly pulling slightly toward you as you roll (stretching).
- Make sure that the roll holds together by sealing the top and the ends and rolling it on the surface gently. Repeat with the second braid. You can mix and match the braids (one with walnut, the other with Turkish delight or mixed fruit) or have both braids the same. Then twist the braids together and place the braids in the pans.
- If you have mixed the fillings before the bulk rise, it is still a good idea to stretch out the dough, roll it, and twist the braids together. This will give you more structure in the babka and a puffier softer texture.

Proving in Pans

- Take the filled pans and place them in plastic bags and let them rise at room temperature for about 2 hours and 30 minutes (or place them in the oven with the oven off and with a small pan of warm water placed at the bottom). They should rise till they double in volume and are just past the lip of the baking pans.
- Egg wash the top of the loaves just before baking (you can sprinkle some Demerara (coarse) sugar on top too).

Baking

- Preheat the oven to 180C (356F) convection (or 381F if you do not have convection). Place the loaves in the center of the oven and bake for 20 minutes. Lower the temperature to 170C (338F) convection (or 364F if you do not have convection) and bake for another 40 minutes. Cover the loaves loosely with parchment paper if they start looking too brown. The toothpick test will not work on walnut filled babkas but may work on raisins or other fillings.
- Take the loaves out of the oven, let cool in pans for about 5 minutes and then remove from pans. Cool on a rack on their side till completely cool. For the first hour or so, switch from one side to the other every 10 to 15 minutes so that the filling does not crush the middle or sides of the dough as it cools.
- Enjoy!

Santa Barbara Persimmon Cake or Pudding (your choice)

Bruce Robertson

Before coming to Santa Barbara I had never lived anywhere in one place longer than 4 years. When we moved in, in December, we inherited a beautiful garden dominated by a large persimmon tree in the backyard. We appreciated the shade all the following summer; and then it started fruiting. And fruiting. And fruiting. It must have produced—and still produces—about 600 persimmons a year, hachiya, the kind you have to let get completely soft to eat, which I don't like eating.

Our neighbors saved us by giving us a page of recipes from the local newspaper. And I have been experimenting with the cake recipe ever since. The persimmon cake has become particularly meaningful because it is a sign of stability and rootedness. I pulp scores of persimmons every year and freeze the pulp until the freezer can't take anymore (this is after I give away bags of them). And then over the holidays, first Thanksgiving and then Christmas, I start baking.

The recipe is pretty free form because my main goal is to get rid of as much of the pulp as possible. So the texture of the cake varies considerably depending on how much pulp I put in—sometimes more like cake, sometimes more like a Christmas pudding—and I never measure the amount, because I'm just defrosting freezer bags with a couple of cups of pulp in each one. But I like the randomness of it, because I am not a baker—I constitutionally cannot consistently measure ingredients.

I think the recipe works well with any soft fruit you can pulp. I'm going to do it with plums this year if we get as big a crop as I think we will.

So this is a recipe about thankfulness. It celebrates a partnership which has lasted happily over thirty years, becoming part of a community, and giving the damn cakes away—we can't possibly eat them all (although they do freeze perfectly well).

It is my personal emblem of Santa Barbara.

Ingredients

- 1 cup sugar
- 1½ sticks butter
- 3 eggs
- 2 tsp vanilla
- 2½ cups all-purpose flour
- 2 tsp baking soda
- ½ tsp salt
- 2 tsp ground allspice
- 2-3 tsp cinnamon
- 2-3 tsp ground ginger
- 2 tsp nutmeg
- 4 cups ripe persimmon pulp
- 2 cups chopped nuts (walnuts or pecans)
- 2 cups dried fruit (dried cherries, golden raisins, chopped dates, etc)
- 2 cups choc chips, semi-sweet

Directions

- The only measurements I measure more or less exactly are the sugar, salt, vanilla, baking soda and flour. The nuts, dried fruit and persimmon I just empty in: the more pulp you use the more pudding-like the texture becomes.

- Start by pulping the persimmons—a very messy process. You pull the skin off with one hand while holding it in the other, and then reach in and pull out the pulp into one bowl and the skin into the other. Freeze it now for later or move on to the next step.

- I am too impatient to wait for butter to reach room temperature so I melt it, and then add it to the sugar, whisk it together, and let it cool a little. While it cools, I beat the eggs lightly, just enough to blend them, and add the vanilla to the eggs, mix lightly, and then add the mixture to the sugar and butter and mix that.

- In a very large bowl, I put the flour and all the spices and mix together. You could sift the spices into the flower but I'm lazy, and just mix them with a spoon.

- Add the butter/sugar/egg mixture and mix until thoroughly mixed. I do it all by hand but you could use a mixer, if you have one big enough.

- Add the persimmon pulp, or whatever fruit pulp you're using. And then add the dried fruit and nuts. Mix well.

- For the pans, I use a random mixture: a set of small non-stick loaf pans, which I grease lightly with oil just to be safe; or two larger bread loaf pans which I grease and line with parchment paper. I find the parchment paper very helpful—it makes getting the loaves out whole much easier. You'll notice I say loaves. This is part of the indeterminacy of the recipe. Loaf pans is what I have. I could probably use cake tins. Sometimes I use a little brownie pan for any leftover dough. But since I almost only ever serve the cake/pudding/bread already cut into slices, I don't care. I just watch it in the oven and when I think it's done I pull it out—sometimes I should have left it in longer, so it's more pudding-y, sometimes I pull it out a little late and it's more cakey.

- Put it in a 350F oven, and bake till done (35min +) depending on what kind of pan you've used, how dry you want it to be, and how brown the top is. I do test it with a toothpick or sharp knife, and if nothing is sticking, then I generally pull it out. (If it gets too brown but it is not done, loosely cover top with parchment paper and bake some more.)

- Let it cool for at least 30 minutes. Then loosen the sides all the way around, invert over a cutting board, and turn out the loaves.

Doey's Apple Cake Pudding from Wynn Speece
Carol Swingle

This simple holiday dessert is easy to make, and great to make ahead of time. Doey is Todd's sister, Dorothy Shields, who introduced this to the family during her first year of marriage. It became a regular for Christmas dinners and was prominently featured in Your Neighbor Lady's stories and cookbooks.

Apple Cake Pudding Ingredients

- 2 cups sugar
- 2 cups flour
- ¼ lb butter
- 2 tsp baking soda
- 2 eggs
- 2 tsp cinnamon
- 4 cups chopped apples, unpeeled
- 1 tsp salt
- 2 tsp nutmeg
- 1 cup chopped nuts (I always use walnuts)

Directions

- Preheat Oven to 325F. Cream sugar and butter in a large mixing bowl. Add eggs. Sift dry ingredients together and add to the beaten mix. This will result in a very stiff batter. Add chopped apples and nuts.
- Beat until well mixed. Pour batter into greased 8"x 8" baking pan.
- Bake at 325F for about an hour until a toothpick comes out clean when inserted in the center.

Hard Sauce Ingredients

- 1 cup sugar
- 1/4 lb butter
- 1 cup half & half
- 1 tsp vanilla extract

Directions

- Combine ingredients in a heavy saucepan and cook over a low heat till slightly thickened. Cook longer to desired thickness.
- For best results, always use real butter.

Basil Gin Gimlet

Marty Spanninger

My favorite summer cocktail made by Mary @ the Red Cat in Chelsea, NYC. On Friday nights after I fed that night's episode of "Now" to PBS stations (John Siceloff '76 was the Executive Producer), I loved going to the Red Cat for dinner at the bar. I met Bob Mueller '68 at our 2006 reunion and he'd join me in NY on Friday nights for the "feed" followed by dinner. When Bob and I married on 6/21/2008 in the Teresa Lang fragrance garden on campus, we served this cocktail to our guests.

- Muddle about 5 basil leaves in ice – crush the ice.
- In covered martini shaker pour 2 oz gin over the ice and muddled basil.
- Add ½ oz fresh squeezed lime juice.
- Add ½ oz simple syrup (made by boiling 1 cup sugar to 1 cup water, chill).
- (Alternatively add 1 oz of frozen limeade concentrate and squeeze in some fresh squeezed lime juice.)
- Add ice to fill.
- Shake VIGOROUSLY.
- Pour/strain into chilled martini glass.
- (Some basil shreds and ice shards will escape and should!)
- Double the recipe for two!

Glogg

Cynthia Rasmussen

Glogg is, in its simplest definition, mulled wine. All Scandinavian countries have their own interpretation of Glogg, but we know the best is Danish Glogg, and we can all agree I'm only slightly biased on this point.

In Danish, there's a term "hygge," which has no direct English translation, but it roughly means coziness. The kind of warm fuzzy feeling or innocent childhood joy (drinking a cup of cocoa after playing with your friends outside while eagerly anticipating opening all of the presents under the tree). That's hygge.

In its broader definition, Glogg is liquid hygge. It'll make you feel warm, cozy and let any worries or problems slip away, if only for a little while. It takes a bunch of simple (read: cheap) ingredients and transforms them into something spectacular.

Don't splurge on expensive wine, port or brandy. Save those to drink them on their own. Also, use whole spices for this, they'll give it that little extra kick that you can't quite place, but know it's just right.

Ingredients

- 750ML bottle of red wine
- Rind of 1 orange
- 1 cinnamon stick (or 2)
- ½ cup of raisins
- ½ cup of blanched almonds
- 10 cardamom pods
- 5 cloves
- ¼ cup honey
- 1 cup of port
- 1 cup brandy

Directions

- Add the wine, orange rind, cinnamon stick(s), raisins, almonds, cardamom seeds, cloves and honey to a pot on the stove.
- Let those simmer (not boil, simmer on low) for at least 30 minutes.
- When you're ready to serve, you can remove the spices if you want (tradition has it that whomever gets a clove wins a prize!), and then add the port and brandy.
- Ladle into mugs and enjoy the hygge.

Class of '76 Garnet Manhattan & Hot Mulled Cider

Marty Spanninger

Class of '76 Garnet Manhattan

- 2 oz Bourbon or Rye (Elijah Craig)
- 1 oz Chambord
- ½ oz Sweet Vermouth (Carpano Antica Formula)
- Dash Walnut Bitters (can substitute any bitters)
- Shake or stir over ice.
- Serve up in a Martini Glass or over ice.
- Garnish with an orange peel and a luxardo cherry.

Class of '76 Hot Mulled Cider — Spicy but Wholesome!

- ½ gallon of fresh, unfiltered apple cider (non-alcoholic)

- 1 orange

- 12 whole cloves

- 4 3-inch sticks of cinnamon

- 15 allspice berries

- ¼ tsp of freshly ground nutmeg

- 7 pods of cardamom

- 2 Tbsp brown sugar (optional)

- Simmer apple cider with orange and spices: Pour apple cider into a 3-quart saucepan, cover, turn the heat on medium-high.

- While cider is heating up, take a vegetable peeler and peel away a couple thick strips of peel from the orange. Press about half of the cloves into the peeled part of the orange. (You can also just quarter the orange and add the slices and cloves separately. I just like seeing the orange bob up and down.)

- Place orange, orange peel strips, the remaining cloves, and the rest of the ingredients into the saucepan with the cider. Keep covered and heat the mulled cider mixture to a simmer and reduce heat to low. Simmer for 20 minutes on low heat.

- Strain out the orange and spices: Use a fine mesh sieve to strain the hot mulled cider away from the orange, cloves, and other spices. If you want, you can add a touch of bourbon, brandy, or rum to spike it up a bit.

- Serve hot. Add a cinnamon stick to each cup if desired.

Lightning Source UK Ltd.
Milton Keynes UK
UKHW022233041221
395025UK00005B/131

9 780578 316451